Choose T… Up

Dear Cllr Joanne Howcroft-Scott,

thank you so much for everything.

Petronela Zilik xxx

Petronela Zilik

Author services including editing by Opulent Books: www.OpulentBooks.net

ISBNS: 978-1-916691-74-2

978-1-916691-75-9

This book is based on the personal life story and experiences of the author. Some names, identifying details, and events have been changed to protect the privacy of individuals. Any resemblance to real persons, living or dead, is coincidental unless explicitly stated.

The information and advice provided in this book are for informational purposes only. The author does not claim to be a licensed professional in trauma counselling, mental health, or related fields. Readers are encouraged to seek professional advice or assistance where necessary.

Table of Contents

Dedication

This book is for all the survivors – those who have faced hard times and still stand strong. You are brave, and your strength is inspiring.

I dedicate this book to anyone who grew up without parents, those who spent their childhood in foster care, and those who were adopted but still held on to the dream of finding their birth parents and uncovering the truth.

This is also for anyone who has lost a parent or grew up without the love and presence of a mother or father. You are not alone, and your story matters.

May this book remind you that hope is never lost, and you are stronger than you realise.

Remember this truth:

"Before I formed you in the womb I knew you."

Jeremiah 1:5

I hope this book gives you hope and courage to keep going.

Endorsements

You can never know the story of a person's life just by looking at them; it must be told, it must be listened to. As you hear 'Part 1' of Petronela's story from these pages, you will be both moved and stirred. Many times, Petronela gave up on herself, but her testimony is this: Jesus never gave up on her. Please make time to read this book; it will be time well spent.

Pastor Chris Gill

Petronela opens her heart and soul in plain sight for everyone to see that, whatever life throws at you, you can overcome it. A truly honest and powerful message of hope for anyone to hold on to, regardless of their hardships. Everyone should read it, as it offers hope to anyone in search of a better life.

Maite Prÿke

I have known Petronela for a very long time. I personally grew up in a foster home, so I know how hard it is to have a childhood like that.

Reading this book made me realise that everything is possible, and it's just up to you to decide which way you want to go. That is why I think you should read this book, to find your way and to know that you are not alone. You can always find help in different ways, whether through God or the people around you.

Viera

Petronela, in this poignant narrative, traces a journey from abandonment and despair to resilience and redemption. Through identity struggles, profound pain, and a transformative turning point, Petronela unveils the triumph of the human spirit. Deeply moving and inspiring, Petronela's writing is a testament to perseverance, healing, and the unwavering power of hope.

Dr. Lady Waynett Peters

The Extraordinary Achievers

Acknowledgements

First and foremost, I offer my heartfelt thanks to my Lord and Saviour, Jesus Christ, for saving my life and being my constant source of strength. I am also deeply grateful to Kings Church Gillingham, Pastor Chris Gill, and his wife Sally for their incredible support over the last three years.

To my dear friends Abigail Nwaeze and Suzzane Lestrade your prayers and encouragement have lifted me more times than I can count. Thank you to Maïté Pryke for believing in me. You have shown me love and support over the past four years, when I needed it most. I will be grateful to you for the rest of my life. Jartua Gilpin, and Jasmine Gilpin, thank you for your positivity and kindness. I am forever grateful to Peter Pastorek, we both have one thing in common: we grew up without parents and carry the same traumas. My brother, my friend, I will forever be grateful to you for a friendship that has lasted over 25 years. It shows just how patient you've been with me. Thank you. You've accepted me for who I am, ever since childhood.. To my great friend Vierka Balazovicova, along with her children Vivien and Jay, for always standing by me.

To my lovely friends Margita Fenzlein, Steve Baxter, Katarina Skutova, Ľubica Krymláková Vláčilová, Silvia Chovancova, and Melania Jamrich and her husband Julius, thank you for the love and support you've shown me. To my amazing mentor, coach, and woman of God, Dr. Waynett Peters, thank you for your strength, inspiration, and humility.

A special thanks to Ingrid Bánska Minarovič and Eliska Durcova for your friendship and light. To my lifelong friend Ivana and my dear friend Petka Fifik, along with her family, your enduring friendship has been a pillar in my life. To my sister in Christ Aldijana Muharemovic thank you for love, prayers and support. Much gratitude to Sovicka - Slovak Children and Youth Folk Group London.

To my adoptive grandmother Maria Hovancova, Miladka and Vierka Kleinova, and my mother, Kvetoslava Vasilova; your love and kindness have anchored me through many storms. My precious children, Massi, David, and Nella, you are my greatest blessings and the reason I continue to persevere.

I am also grateful to Eva Neuwirathová for 15 years of unwavering friendship, and to my friends from Bulgaria, Ramis Ramis and Ruslana Uzunova, for embracing me as I am. To Beata Hrickova and all the carers from the orphanage, I will always be grateful. Sophie Godwin, my lovely and beautiful sister in Christ, always ready to pray for me. Thank you so much.

To Luise and Tim Ringrose, thank you for your hospitality and generosity during a critical time in my life. I will always be grateful for the stability and kindness you provided. Petra Gaziova (JPR Connections) and Raymond Dunsks, thank you so much for your support!

To Danka Klamparova Bowcott and her husband Richard, along with Neil Charlick from The Street Angels Gillingham, thank you for your support with Petronela's Hope. To Pastor James Sowah, Mrs. Sandra Sowah, Pastor Seun Oyedele, and his wife Hannah, your spiritual guidance and prayers have been a blessing on this journey.

To Pastor Joe Benjamin, I am deeply thankful for your guidance and encouragement throughout the writing process. This book would not have been possible without your support.

Finally, to everyone who has touched my life, whether in big or small ways, I am truly grateful. Your love, kindness, and support have shaped this book and my journey, and I dedicate this to you all.

Introduction

I am writing this book because I believe my story can help others. My life has not been easy. It has been filled with countless rejections and struggles I wouldn't wish on anyone. But through it all, I have learnt one thing: no matter how hard life gets, we must choose to never give up.

I was abandoned as a baby, abused as a child, and spent years feeling unwanted and unloved. For a long time, I believed I did not matter. I thought my life was just one mistake after another. I lived with anger, shame, and a deep emptiness that no one could fill. There were times I wanted to give up completely, and more than once, I tried to end my life. But somehow, I kept going. I clung to the hope that there was something more for me, a reason for all the pain.

If you are reading this, maybe you have felt the same. Maybe you have gone through abuse, battled mental health struggles, or felt lost in life. Maybe you have looked at your situation and thought, "I do not know how to carry on." Let me tell you something: you are not alone. I have been there too.

This book is for the survivors, the ones who have been through the worst but are still here. It is for the single mothers trying to hold everything together, the people wrestling with trauma or addiction, and those searching for answers in the darkest moments of life. It is for anyone who feels like giving up but, deep down, still wants to believe there is hope.

I am sharing my story because I have seen what happens when you keep going, even when it feels impossible. I have seen how God can take the broken pieces of your life and create something beautiful. There is a reason for your pain, even if you cannot see it right now. And I promise, you are not as alone as you think.

The title, Choose to Never Give Up (Book 1), reflects

my life. Every day, I have had to make that choice. As a child, I endured physical, emotional, and sexual abuse. I ran away from home, lived in forests, and befriended rats because they felt safer than people. I was homeless, battling addiction, and searching for my mother, only to be rejected by her when I finally found her. Each time, I had to dig deep and find the strength to keep going. Each time, I learnt something new about resilience, hope, and the God who was with me all along.

The turning point for me came when I was ready to give up completely. I had hit rock bottom. I was broken and desperate. But in that moment, I felt God's love for the first time. It was like nothing I had ever experienced before. I realised I was not a mistake, I was not unloved, and my life mattered. That moment changed everything.

Through this book, I want to share that same hope with you. I want you to see that healing is possible. It is not easy, and it does not happen overnight, but it is worth the journey. I have learnt that healing starts with admitting you are damaged, accepting help, and trusting that God has a plan for you. It is okay to feel weak. It is okay to feel lost.

But you do not have to stay there.

As you read this book, you will hear about the darkest moments of my life, the abuse, the mistakes, and the years of struggling with self-worth. But you will also hear about the moments of redemption, the people who showed me kindness, and the God who never gave up on me, even when I wanted to give up on myself.

This is more than a story; it is a message of hope. I want you to see that no matter what you have been through, there is a way forward. There is a God who loves you and wants to heal you. And if you let Him, He can take the pain, the brokenness, and the mistakes, and turn them into something beautiful.

So, to the survivors, the single mothers, the ones struggling in silence, and anyone who feels like giving up, this book is for you. I hope it gives you the courage to keep going. I hope it reminds you that you are not alone. And most of all, I hope it helps you see that with God, nothing is impossible.

This is just part one of my story, part two is in another book. Let us choose to never give up.

CHAPTER 1

Abandoned Beginnings

I was born on the 6th of October, 1984, in Slovakia. How I came into this world is surrounded by mystery and stories that don't quite add up. Some say I was found outside in a basket, while others say I was discovered in a plastic bag. Either way, the beginning of my life was marked by rejection. I didn't have the warm embrace of a mother or the protective arms of a father. By the time I was two months old, I had been taken into an orphanage. My first home wasn't a family, it was an institution.

The orphanage was a place where children without parents were sent to live. There were about 40 of us, each with a different story but the same hurt. Each of us longed for the same thing: a family. We wanted someone to choose us, to take us into their home, to love us as their own. We were all waiting for that special day when it would finally be our turn to leave the orphanage. For some, that day came quickly. But for me, the waiting felt endless.

My earliest memory is from when I was four years old. I remember sitting alone, asking myself the same question over and over: "Where is my mum? Where is my mother?" I didn't know who she was, what she looked like, or where she might be. But deep down, I believed she was out there. I told myself that one day, she would come for me, and we would be together forever. That hope became my escape. Whenever life became unbearable, I would picture her in my mind and imagine the day she would hold me and tell me she loved me.

When I turned four, I was moved into a foster family. At the time, I didn't know what a foster family was. All I knew was that I was being taken away from the orphanage to live with people who were supposed to take care of me. I thought maybe this was my chance to finally feel loved and safe. But that hope didn't last long.

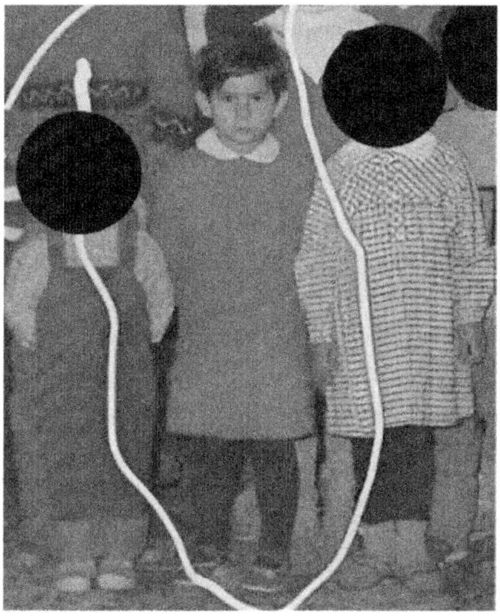

The foster home wasn't a safe place. It became a place of confusion. My foster father began what he called "games." He tied my hands and feet to the bed and said it was just for fun. His wife, who drank heavily, would sit nearby and watch, doing nothing to stop him. I didn't understand what was happening – I was only a child. I was scared, but at the same time, I craved their attention. These "games" became the only way I felt noticed.

It got worse. I was forced to sleep naked next to him. He made me touch him in ways I didn't understand. If I refused, I was punished by not being fed. I was so young, so confused, and I didn't have anyone to protect me. At some point, I started to believe that this was normal – that this was just the way life was. But deep down, I knew something wasn't right. When it became too much, I would close my eyes and imagine my mother. I pictured her coming to rescue me, taking me far away from the discomfort. That thought became my comfort – my only escape.

Life in the foster home left scars that stayed with me for years. I remember hiding under the bed, crying until I could barely breathe. But even then, I made sure no one saw my tears. I had learnt early on that showing weakness only made things worse. I became a master at hiding my emotions. No one would ever see my pain, even though it was tearing me apart inside.

As I grew older, I began to dread the holidays. The breaks were supposed to be a happy time, but for me, they meant going back to my foster parents, back to the place where I felt trapped and powerless. I hated it so much that I started screaming and punching myself in front of my carers, hoping they would think I was too difficult to handle and send me somewhere else. But they didn't understand my behaviour. They thought I was just being a troublemaker. No one stopped to ask why I was acting that way or what I was going through.

I was sent back to orphanage because of bad behaviour. The orphanage was filled with children like me, children who had been abandoned or taken from their families. Each of us carried our own pain, but we shared the same dream. We all wanted to be chosen. We all wanted a family. But as the years passed, I realised that some of us were forgotten, left behind, while others got to leave and start a new life.

Even at that young age, I knew my life was different from other children's. I didn't have the love and care that every child deserves. My childhood was filled with rejection, abuse, and loneliness. But despite everything, I held on to one thing: the hope that my mother was out there somewhere. I believed that everything would be okay if I could find her. That hope, fragile as it was, became my reason to keep going.

Looking back now, I realise how much that hope carried me through the darkest moments. It gave me something to hold on to when everything else felt like it was falling apart. My childhood was far from normal, but it shaped me into the person I am today. And even though it was filled with agony, it also taught me to fight, to survive, and to never give up.

Life in the orphanage was often a strange mix of hope and heartbreak. Whenever people came to adopt a child, the staff would make us dress up in our best clothes. We had to be on our best behaviour, smiling as if nothing was wrong, and pretending we were perfect children. The idea was simple: if we looked happy, behaved well, and appeared lovable, someone might choose us.

I disliked those days. Deep down, I didn't want to be chosen by strangers. I wanted my mother to come for me. Each time a couple walked through the doors, I wondered if she might be one of them. But she never came. That realisation filled me with a mixture of sadness and anger that I didn't know how to handle.

As a child, I hated dolls. They seemed pointless to me, so I started tearing their heads off. It was almost like I wanted to destroy the happiness they represented, happiness I couldn't feel. When I got a teddy bear, I would pull it apart, ripping out the stuffing, and then throw it in the bin. But some nights, I felt so alone that I would pick up one of the broken toys and hold it close as I fell asleep. Even though I destroyed them, they were the only things I had to cling to in those lonely moments.

I was sent to different foster families four times. Each time, they sent me back to the orphanage, saying I was unmanageable, calling me a difficult child. It felt like every move confirmed what I already believed: that no one wanted me, not even the people who were supposed to give me a home. The rejection hurt, but it also made me stubborn. I started acting out, doing things on purpose so that no one would take me again. If no one wanted me, then I would stay in the orphanage where at least I knew what to expect.

One memory from that time has stayed with me like a

scar that never fades. One day, seven older boys (teenagers) cornered me in the bathroom, I was six years old at the time. They stripped me naked, mocking me, laughing at how no one wanted me. They told me I was worthless, that I was nothing. One of them said, "Even your own mother didn't want you."

They said they were going to "play" with me, and in that moment, I felt terrified and helpless. But something in me snapped. I kicked one of the boys between the legs as hard as I could, grabbed a towel, and ran away. I ran until I found a hiding spot, trembling with fear. Later, the boy I kicked found me and said, "If you tell anyone, no one will believe you. There are seven of us, and only one of you. You're just a liar. You're no one. No one wanted you, not even your mother."

His words hit me harder than his threats. I already believed them to be true. I felt like nothing – a child who didn't matter to anyone. I crawled under my bed that night, clutching my broken dolls, and cried silently. I couldn't let anyone see my tears. In the dark, I started punching the headless dolls, imagining they were the boys and that I was fighting back. But even then, my thoughts drifted to my mother. I help on to the hope that one day she would come and prove them wrong.

As I hid under the bed clutching the headless dolls, I felt so many emotions at once. One moment, I punched them in anger, imagining I was fighting off the boys who had mocked me. The next, I found myself hugging the fragmented toys tightly, pretending they were someone who cared for me. I didn't mind that the dolls didn't have heads. At least, they were something I could hold. They were all I had.

Even in those moments, my thoughts always drifted to my mother. I wondered what she was doing, what she was eating, and whether she ever thought about me. Did she miss me? Did she wonder if I was safe? I created stories in my head to comfort myself, imagining that she loved me and wanted me, but for some reason, couldn't find me. Thinking about her became my way of coping. Whenever life felt unbearable, I told myself that one day, I would find her, and we would be together forever.

Christmas at the Orphanage

Christmas at the orphanage was meant to be a happy time. We received so many presents, and the carers showed us extra love and attention. But it was always a sad time for me. No matter how many gifts I opened, my mother was never there. Each time I tore the wrapping paper, my heart hoped for something magical, something that would bring her back to me. But it was always just toys or clothes. I would look at them for a moment, then throw them aside because they didn't matter. Nothing mattered if my mother wasn't there.

I still remember one of the carers, a woman named Beata, who worked at the orphanage during that time. To me, she was the most beautiful woman in the world. Her kind smile could lit up a room, and whenever she sat me on her lap to read me a story, I felt special. I felt chosen. Beata had so much patience with me, even when I was disobedient and difficult. She never shouted at me or made me feel bad about myself. Instead, she would smile, look into my eyes, and give me a hug. For those brief moments,

I felt safe, loved, and seen.

But even with her kindness, there was a great sadness at Christmas. It wasn't just me who felt it – all the children did. We all longed for the same thing: to be with our mothers. No number of presents could fill that empty space in our hearts.

As a child, I spent so much time dreaming about my mother. I would take a piece of paper and draw hearts all over it, over and over again. In the middle of each heart, I would write, "I miss you, Mum." Sometimes, I would draw pictures of myself standing next to her, hand in hand. I believed she was looking for me, just like I was waiting for her. I believed she loved me and that one day, we would find each other and never be apart again.

Drawing those pictures gave me hope. It was my way of saying, "I love you, Mum," even though I didn't know if she could hear me. I filled the paper with hearts, over and over again, as if the more I drew, the closer I would be to finding her.

After a while, I realised that life at the orphanage wasn't

all negative. I didn't like the food, especially the bread and jam, but I loved the friendships I had there. The other children became like a family to me. We shared the same tears and the same longing for parents we didn't have. We were all survivors, bound together by our loss.

Even with my friends, I couldn't understand why my mother wasn't with me. I didn't understand why she wasn't there to hold me during Christmas or why I couldn't be with her like other children were with their families. It was a question that stayed with me every day, one I couldn't answer no matter how much I dreamed or hoped.

I wanted to leave the institution, but because of this hope, I started behaving better at the orphanage. I told myself that if I was well-behaved, someone might adopt me, and I could escape the boys who tormented me. The day finally came when I heard that a family had chosen me. I was thrilled and hopeful. This was my chance to start over, to have a new life with a new family.

A New Family: My Adoption at Eight

I had a glimpse of my future adoptive parents for the first time when they came to the orphanage. I was very happy that they chose me, but also confused because they chose both me and another girl, a nine-year-old called Martina. We went to their home for the holidays.

Martina was like a sister to me. We had one thing in common: we had both been unwanted since we were little, a shared pain that we kept hidden.

After two weeks, without me knowing at the time, Martina was sent back to the orphanage while I was kept. I felt sad and confused. I did not understand why I would not see her again or why they had not chosen both of us.

Later, I heard that my adoptive parents refused to keep her because she had taken a lipstick without permission. I remember telling her, "Give it back!" but she did not listen. The next day, she was gone.

And so, I started living in a new home, but I really missed having a sister by my side, someone to play with and talk to throughout my childhood.

I was eight years old at the time I was adopted. Social services introduced me to this couple and told me, "This is your new mother and father." I remember staring at them and thinking, *Where have you been all this time?* They told me to call them Mum and Dad, and I obeyed, even though it felt strange. I was determined to do everything they asked of me because I didn't want to go back to the orphanage. I wanted to be the perfect child, no matter how hard it was.

But the happiness didn't last. As soon as social services left, my mother slapped me. She told me I had to stop saying that she wasn't my real mother. I had called her a liar, and she didn't like that. From that moment, things got worse. The beatings became a regular part of my life until the age of eighteen.

She beat me so often that I lost count. Sometimes it was two or three times a week, usually in the mornings before school or after I came home. If I cried, it only made things worse. She would hit me harder, shouting at me to stop crying. So, I made a promise to myself: I would never cry in front of her again. I would become like stone, silent and unbreakable.

People saw what was happening. Neighbours, relatives, even strangers witnessed how she abused me, but no one stepped in to help. They just watched or walked away as if it wasn't their problem. One time, she beat me so badly that my nose wouldn't stop bleeding. My aunt was there, but instead of helping, she just left. My father also stood by and did nothing. No one defended me. No one protected me.

Eventually, I told someone what was happening. I told them how my mother hit me and hurt me, and social services came back. They wanted to take me away, back to the orphanage. At first, I thought it might be a relief to leave, but deep down, I was scared of the boys and the loneliness. So, I stayed quiet and pretended everything was fine.

Looking back, I can see how those years shaped me. They taught me to hide my pain, to never show weakness, and to rely only on myself. I learned that the people who were supposed to care for me could not always be trusted.

And yet, even in the darkest moments, I held on to the hope that my mother was out there, waiting for me. It was that hope that kept me going.

I didn't want to return to the orphanage, so I lied to social services. I told them I had made everything up, that I was a liar. I even said the bruises on my body were my own doing, as if I had somehow caused them to appear. In my mind, the fear of being sent back to that foster family where I had been sexually abused was worse than staying where I was.

After I convinced them that I was lying, they left. But the humiliation wasn't over. My mother made me kneel in front of her, pleading for forgiveness. I begged her not to send me away. I promised I would do whatever she wanted, as long as she let me stay. She eventually said yes, but the moment we got home, everything fell apart again.

My father went out drinking, as he often did, leaving me alone with her. She wasted no time in showing me exactly how much she despised me. She beat me again, this time harder than before. I think she wanted to make sure I would never tell anyone about what was happening in our house.

One time, during one of her beatings, I told her that I didn't feel anything. I smiled at her, even though my body was screaming in agony. Her anger exploded – she grabbed a wooden stick and struck me repeatedly. I refused to show any emotion. I sat there on the chair, silent and still, as though none of it affected me. On the outside, I looked unbothered. But on the inside, I was breaking apart.

I hated going home. Every morning, I ran to school with joy, feeling free for a little while. I loved school because it was the only place where I could be free from her troubles. But as the school day came to an end, my heart would sink. I walked home as slowly as I could, dragging my feet, wishing I didn't have to go back.

When I was about 9, a schoolmate told me, "You were found in a basket, and no one wanted you. You're an orphan." Her words filled me with rage. I slapped her and shouted, "My mother wanted me! I will find her!" After that, I became more violent at school. I started beating boys and lashing out at anyone who crossed me. Inside, though, I was just broken. I felt so angry and so hopeless.

The only person who knew what was really happening was my best friend, Ivana. She was my lifeline in those dark days. I told her everything about the beatings, the abuse, and how hopeless I felt. Ivana was the first person in my life who truly listened to me. She couldn't do much to help, since she was just a child herself, but her kindness meant everything to me. She made me feel like I wasn't completely alone.

Ivana couldn't change my situation, but she gave me something that no one else did: understanding. Just by listening to me, she helped me carry the weight of everything I was going through. In a world where most people either ignored or added to my pain, she stood out as a small light in the darkness.

Those early years of my life were filled with rejection and fear. Every day felt like a battle to survive, and every night, I lay awake wishing for something better. The abuse at home, the feelings of being unwanted, and the constant hope for my mother shaped my entire childhood. I learnt to stay silent, to hide my tears, and to endure.

But even in the darkest moments, there was a part of me that refused to give up. I didn't know how to escape, and I didn't know if things would ever change, but I kept holding on. Somewhere deep inside, I believed that there was more to life than this, even if I hadn't seen it yet.

Reflections: God, the Father to the Fatherless

Looking back, I now see that even in the darkest moments of rejection and loneliness, God was always there. He is the Father to the fatherless, the One who steps in when the world turns away. For those of us who have felt abandoned, unloved, or forgotten, God offers something no one else can which is a love that never fails.

The Bible tells us in Psalm 68:5, "A father of the fatherless, a defender of widows, is God in His holy habitation" (NKJV). This truth is for everyone who has felt the burden of not having a parent to guide or love them. God sees your tears, and He knows your struggles.

Even when others have turned their backs on you, God has always been there, waiting with open arms to comfort and protect you.

Rejection can leave wounds that feel impossible to heal. It can make you feel unworthy, like you do not belong. But God's Word reminds us that this is not the end of the story.

If you feel lost, remember that God's love is constant. He is the parent you have been searching for, the One who will never leave you. You are not alone. You are not rejected. God's love is stronger than any pain or rejection you have experienced. Open your heart to Him and let Him show you how deeply He cares for you. You are His, and His love will never let you go.

Story of One Girl

I tell you a story of one girl,
She lost her mama and papa.
Everyone used her, just for their games,
No one knew the pain.

I tell you a story of one girl,
She hid her tears under the bed.

When she stood next to the ones who should love her,
Love was shown through fighting and screaming.
She believed she was evil from a young age,
At least she was something – because of fear.
The girl became like a stone,
She couldn't stand up for herself.

I tell you a story of one girl,
Only God knows how many nights she cried.
Her dreams were a joke to others,
But she just wanted her mum next to her.

She became braver and more stubborn,
Yet she believed she was a mistake from the moment she was born.
She told herself, "One day will come."

She was always pleasing others,
"Love me, I'm just a child,
How God created me." Please, please somebody love me,
I'm just a child."

CHAPTER 2

Childhood in the Shadows

One day, I heard my father calling me. "Petronela! Come here, let's go for a walk."

I froze for a moment, not sure if he was talking to me. When I peeked around the corner, he was standing there, smiling, with his hand stretched out towards me. "Come on," he said again, his voice soft and kind.

Slowly, I walked over and placed my hand in his. It felt strange but comforting. He led me down the road, and for the very first time, it was just the two of us. The sun was warm, and everything felt calm. When we stopped for ice cream, I couldn't help but smile as I licked the cold sweetness, looking up at him. For that one afternoon, I felt like a normal little girl, loved and safe. I held onto that feeling tightly, not knowing it would soon slip away. That day was the best day ever.

My father was one of the only things I loved in that house. But those moments with him were rare. He worked far away as a painter and only came home once a month. The rest of the time, I was left alone with my mother, and during those days, she became a monster. Whenever she and my father fought, she blamed me for everything. "It's all your fault," she would scream. "You are the reason for all of this." She called me names like "devil child" and told me over and over that I was nothing. Eventually, I started to believe her.

One time, after a fight with my mother, my father locked himself in the garage and turned on the gas. I can still remember the smell. Screaming with rage, she grabbed an axe and smashed the door down. He came out drunk and stumbling, and she made me stand there and watch it all. "This is your fault," she said, dragging me inside the house afterwards. She put him to bed and then turned her anger back to me, beating me until I couldn't stand.

There were moments when my father tried to defend me. I remember one day he told her, "You should stop beating Petronela." I was so shocked, I could hardly believe it. For once, someone was standing up for me. But that didn't last long. His drinking got worse after that, and the fights became even more violent. Sometimes, he would throw plates in anger, smashing them against the table or the walls. One day, he even threw a plate at me.

By the time I was ten years old, he slapped me for the first time. It was so hard that I fell to the floor and saw nothing but darkness. Later that night, I went to bed, only for my mother to come in and beat me again. Every time she finished, I had to tell her, "It's my fault. I'm sorry." Only then would she leave me alone.

But some nights, she would come back. Sometimes, she would sit beside me, crying, and tell me she loved me. I was so confused – how could she beat me so cruelly and then say she loved me? It didn't make sense. I never asked her why. I just stayed quiet, trying to understand something that felt impossible to figure out.

When I made her angry, she would punish me by locking me in a dark room all day with no food. I was always hungry as a child. When I asked her for food, she would refuse, so I started stealing food at night while they slept. I would hide bread under my bed or in my pockets. But when she found out, she beat me even more.

In the dark, I found comfort in the mice that scurried around the room. They became my friends. I would talk to them quietly, feeling like they were the only ones who listened.

One Christmas, she cooked chicken soup, and I told her I had had enough. She slapped me repeatedly and forced me to sit at the table until I finished every last bite. I felt so sick, and eventually, I vomited. But that didn't stop her. She grabbed my neck and made me eat my vomit. That moment is stuck into my memory.

I often asked my mother why she adopted me if she hated me so much. Her response was always the same: a slap across the face, followed by insults. "You should be grateful we took you in," she said. When I told her I hadn't asked to be adopted, she beat me even harder.

She always told me I would never amount to anything. "You're the worst child ever," she would say. "You will never be a mother. You will never be anything." One day, I gathered the courage to tell her, "I'd rather be nothing than be like you." That only made her angrier, and the beatings became worse.

I don't remember her ever saying, "Well done," or, "You did something right." Every mistake, every bad thing that happened, was always my fault. I started to believe it. I believed I was a mistake, that I wasn't supposed to exist.

Eventually, I didn't want to be myself anymore. I wanted to be someone else – anyone but me.

Saved by the Doorbell

My mother had a way of making every beating feel like a punishment for simply existing. Most of the time, she hit me on the head. She would grab my neck and force me to sit in a chair. "Don't move," she would say, but if I did, she would throw me to the floor and hit me harder. She used whatever was closest to her – whether it was wooden sticks, shoes, belts, or her bare hands.

She always punched with her right hand, heavy and relentless. The pain was sharp, but strangely, it began to disappear. I didn't understand why I couldn't feel it anymore. Every time she did this, I heard a strange buzzing in my head, and eventually, I would fall asleep from the exhaustion.

I began to think there was something wrong with me. Was I crazy? Why didn't I feel it the way I should? Once, I tried to explain it to her. "I don't feel anything," I told her as she assaulted me. She slapped me harder and screamed, "You feel nothing? I'll make you feel something!" But still, I felt nothing. This only made her angrier. She found heavier sticks, aiming for my legs and arms as I tried desperately to protect my head.

One day, she struck me so hard that blood poured from my ears and nose. It wouldn't stop. My face was covered, and I couldn't breathe properly. Afterwards, she grabbed a cloth and tried to wash the blood from my face. Her hands were rough, and when she finished, she slapped me again about three or four times. Blood splattered everywhere, but she didn't stop.

Then the doorbell rang. I froze, hoping it was someone who could help me. My mother hissed, "Be quiet," and opened the door. It was my adoptive grandmother, my father's mother.

She was a lovely woman, kind and gentle, and when she saw me, her face changed. "What are you doing?" she cried. "Stop! Stop beating her!"

But my mother was furious. "This is none of your business!" she screamed, slamming the door in her face. I stood there, trembling, blood still dripping from my nose. She turned back to me and hit me again.

Another day, the doorbell rang again. My heart raced as I heard my mother shouting, but this time, my grandmother forced her way inside. "I've had enough," she said. "You need to stop this."

That moment was a blessing. She stopped hitting me,

and I was able to crawl into bed and hide under it. My grandmother's visit gave me a small moment of peace, and for that, I was so grateful.

But it didn't end there. My mother and grandmother had a terrible fight. She cursed at her, screamed, and eventually kicked her out of the house. I will never forget the way my grandmother looked at me before she left. Her eyes were filled with pain and helplessness. She wanted to save me, but she didn't know how.

As she stood at the door, I shouted, "Don't worry, Grandma! I'm fine, really!" But we both knew I wasn't. She gave me one last look and then walked away.

That moment stayed with me. It was the first time someone had tried to stand up for me, even if they couldn't win. For a brief moment, I felt seen, and for that, I will always be grateful to her.

Unnoticed Gestures of Love

I think I was 11 years old when I wanted to surprise my mother for Mother's Day. I made a card for her by hand,

and on the way home, I picked some flowers from someone else's garden to go with it. I was so happy and excited, thinking she would be pleased with my effort.

When I got home, I smiled and said, "Mum, I made something for you." I handed her the flowers, expecting her to be happy. Instead, she grabbed me by the neck and slapped me. She shouted, "You didn't even spend any money on me. You just stole these flowers!"

She threw the flowers in the bin and didn't even open the card I had made, tossing it in as well. I stood there, frozen and ashamed. I whispered, "I'm sorry, I'm so sorry." But she slapped me again, and I quietly went back to my room.

I detested myself for what had happened. After that day, I never tried to make anything for her again. I always tried to please my parents, to show them I was grateful they had adopted me, even though I hadn't asked for it. But no matter what I did, they were never satisfied.

I tried so hard to be a good girl, but they always found mistakes in everything I did. If something went wrong, even by accident, they never believed me. They always blamed me for everything. I had to control even the way I breathed or walked around her. I was constantly on edge, frozen in fear.

Over time, I started believing I was an evil child. Sometimes, I hit or slapped myself, thinking I deserved it. I wanted so badly to show them that I loved them, but it never seemed to matter.

For example, with the flowers, I had just wanted to show her how much I cared, but instead, it ended in more punishment. I felt so stupid and blamed myself, slapping my own face and saying, "Why am I so stupid?"

Deep in my heart, I believed that only my real mother would love me for who I was. That thought gave me hope. It gave me the strength to wait and survive all of this because I believed one day, I would find her.

Zahurawood

I was around 12 years old when I finally built up the courage to share a secret I had been holding onto for years with my mother. I took a deep breath, inhaling and exhaling slowly, determined to stay brave. Before joining my adopted family, I had spent time in an orphanage. Prior to that, I was with a foster family. It was there that a man hurt me. He touched me, tied me to the bed, and forced me to sleep next to him.

I hoped that by telling her, she would help me or at least listen. But instead, she slapped me hard across the face and hit me in the stomach with a pestle. "You're a liar," she spat. "You have made this up".

I felt the sting of her words as deeply as the pain of her blows. That day, I learned a painful lesson: trusting her was a mistake. I never told her, or anyone else about my secret again. I carried it alone, trapped by the fear that no one would believe me.

After that, I began running away from their house as often as I could. It wasn't just to escape the abuse; it was to escape the shame and guilt that had taken root inside me. I stopped trusting my parents.

My parents installed a fence outside my room to stop

me from running away. But I found a way out anyway. I started running away to escape them, and every time I did, I felt so free. I would head straight to the forest, to a beautiful place called Zahurawood in Spišské Vlachy, Slovakia. The forest became my safe place.

Whenever I found myself there, I imagined I was a bird. I would stretch out my arms like wings, wishing I could fly. I wanted to fly far away to find my mother. I believed she wanted me – that she was searching for me too. I told my best friend, Ivana, "One day I will find my mother. She definitely wants me. She's looking for me. I know it." I clung to that belief because it was all I had.

My adopted parents, and even some people in the

village, started calling me "jungle girl" because I ran away so often. I told them, "Yes, I am a monkey," pretending to agree. Most people had no idea what I was going through. They thought I was just crazy. I let them believe that because it was easier than explaining. Sometimes I cried because no one truly saw me. They didn't know the real pain I carried or what was happening at home.

At home, my mother always painted me as a troublemaker. She said I was the problem, and I believed her. At school, I lied a lot. I made up stories because I wanted someone to listen to me. Lying was the only way I could get attention.

I loathed weekends because I would be locked in the basement or my room. My mother and father never asked me how I was or how my day had been. They never asked what I wanted or needed. As a child, I loved playing football, but they never let me join in. So, I lied. I told her I was going to an art or dance club, but instead, I joined a football club. For six months, I played without her knowing. When she found out, she beat me and refused to give me dinner.

Forest Fairy

I love the scent of the forest.
In my dreams, I dance
Like a forest fairy, free,
With no one to stop me.
The smile of the sun warms my soul,
Filling my mind with peace.
But the storm and rain approach,
And the forest fairy trembles,
With nowhere to hide,
Her fear grows wild.
Her home is every tree,
Her voice speaks through dreams.
She longs for arms to hold her,
For someone to love her.
The forest wind gently combs her hair,
The moon becomes her pillow,
The grass, a cold duvet.
She knows she must live alone,
Lost in a world without love.
She climbs her favourite tree,
And with a heavy heart,
She lets go,
Believing her final breath has come.
But her eyes open once more.
Disappointment fills her heart.
She realises she is still alive.

Reading became my escape. I loved Jules Verne's books and read them several times. His stories gave me a sense of adventure and hope. Inspired by them, I started writing poems.

My fear of my mother was constant. Sometimes, when she shouted at me, I would wet myself because I was so scared. This only made her angrier. She would beat me for it or slap me hard. I felt so ashamed. To stop myself, I started putting toilet paper in my underwear. When she discovered this, she screamed at me, asking why I was doing it. Her anger terrified me, and I forced myself to try harder not to wet myself. But most of the time, I couldn't make it to the toilet in time, and it only made her more furious.

Sometimes my parents would leave me alone for two or three days. They locked me in the house, but those were the best times for me. I knew I wouldn't be beaten, at least for a little while. I spent those days reading my books in peace. I wasn't allowed to watch TV, have friends, or speak to anyone, but in those quiet moments, I felt free.

My mother was unpredictable. Some nights, she would come into my room at midnight, hug me, and say, "I love you." Then she would ask, "Why are you such a bad child?" Her words made me feel so small. I cried and apologised from the bottom of my heart, saying, "I'm sorry for everything. I know I am a bad child." She would reply, "Yes, you are, and no one will love you if you behave like this."

I believed her. I believed I was unlovable, and worthless. I never dared to ask her or my father any questions. I played by myself most of the time, playing cards or chess. I loved chess because I always won.

A particular Christmas, I received a doll as a present. I cut its hair, stripped it of its clothes, and started sleeping next to it, naked. That doll became my comfort, my companion in the loneliness of that house.

Reflections: Hope in the Midst of Pain

Even in the darkest moments of life, when it feels like the world has turned against you, there is a light that never goes out. For those who have experienced abuse, rejection, or deep loneliness, it is easy to believe the lies spoken over you like you are unworthy, unloved, or a mistake. But these are not truths; they are chains meant to hold you down.

The Bible tells us in Psalm 34:18, "The Lord is near to those who have a broken heart, and saves such as have a contrite spirit" (NKJV). This is a promise that God sees your pain, He hears your cries, and He is close to you, even when it feels like no one else is. His love is constant, unshaken, and never dependent on what others think or say about you. He will not forget you. He holds you in the palm of His hand, knowing your worth and purpose.

Take heart in this truth: You are not defined by the actions of others or by the words spoken over you. You are deeply loved, treasured, and created with a purpose by God Himself. When the pain feels unbearable, reach out to Him. He is near, ready to comfort, heal, and restore.

I'm a Survivor, I'm a Hero

I know what life is about,
Walking through the darkness.
I know what it feels like
When there seems to be no hope.
I know what it's like to think,
When your mind whispers to die.
I know what it's like
Trying to cope with drugs and run away.
No, no more. I'm not a slave to your acts.
I'm a survivor, I'm a hero.
Thanks to God, I'm still alive.
No, no more. I'm not a slave to your acts.
I'm a survivor, I'm a hero.
I choose to forgive you – so goodbye to your acts.
I know what it's like not to love yourself,
Because someone stole your innocence
With their violence and their rape.
I know. I hear you.
I want to stand for you.
Please, never give up.
I know. I hear you.
I want to cry with you.
I understand your pain – I've experienced it too.
You are not alone. I will cry with you.
Please, never give up.

CHAPTER 3

Seeking Identify and Safety

There was a day I ran straight to the school toilets before class began. I shut the door and cried quietly, making sure no one could hear or see me. The load on my chest was so heavy, and I couldn't hold it in anymore. My mother had beaten me again that morning, and I was so angry. I wanted to scream, but I didn't know how. I kept asking myself, *Why is this happening to me? How can I prove to someone that she is hurting me?*

One day, the opportunity came when the school announced that all the children would be going for a medical check-up with the GP. I made a plan. I thought, *This is my chance to show someone the truth.* That evening, I heated up an iron and pressed it against my skin. I also bit myself, leaving marks on my arms and legs. I didn't feel the pain. I never did. It only made me more convinced that something was wrong with me. *Am I crazy? Why can't I feel anything?* I was only ten years old, and I had already started to believe I was crazy. I felt like a very strange child who didn't belong on this planet. Even when I was bitten, I didn't feel any pain.

The next day, during the check-up, I told the doctor that my mother was beating me. I thought this was it. I thought someone would finally believe me – that someone would save me. The doctor contacted social services, my parents, and even some people from our community. For a brief moment, I felt hope, but it didn't last. My mother convinced everyone that she was innocent, and when they confronted me, I said, *Yes, I lied.* I was scared, and in that moment, I gave up my truth.

From that day, everyone called me a liar. And strangely, I liked it. At least, I had their attention. For once, I wasn't invisible. I told my best friend Ivana what I had done, how I had made up the bruises because I wanted to prove that she was hurting me. But I had no evidence, so I created my own.

When we went home that evening, my mother was furious. She beat me again, harder than ever before. I had damaged her name, and she hated me even more for it. I felt hopeless, like I could never win. But at the same time, a part of me felt happy. Being called a liar was better than being nothing. I was getting more afraid of her all these years. Whenever she came close to me, my heart would start beating like crazy. Deep down, I was so scared of her all the time, but I learned not to show it.

Friends in the Wild

I loved spending time with my grandmother. She always had a warm smile, beautiful blue eyes, and a kindness that made me feel safe. She would secretly hide chocolate in her apron pocket and give it to me when no one was looking. I would save it until the evening, eating it quietly in my bed while tears ran down my face. I thought about my mother as I ate, wondering where she was and if she was thinking about me.

My grandmother was unique, unlike anyone else in my life. She never raised her voice or complained about anything. She was always peaceful, her face always wore a smile. She devoted her to prayer and listened attentively to me when I needed to speak. She made me feel valued and important. I loved being with her, and as I got older, I started running away just to see her.

The Zahurawood forest, which became my refuge, was about six miles from me. I often stayed there overnight, alone but never afraid. The wild animals felt like my friends, and I felt safer there than I ever did at home. The trees, the animals, and the quiet of the forest gave me a sense of freedom I couldn't find anywhere else.

One day, I met a snake in the forest. It slithered close to me, and for a moment, I frozen with fear. But before I could move, a wolf appeared and jumped on the snake, saving me. I couldn't believe it – I was so grateful. Later, I snuck into the village, stole some bread, and brought it back to the wolf as a thank you. He was still there, waiting.

I gave him all the food, even though I was starving. I didn't care. I was just so thankful for what he had done.

Over time, more animals came to me. A wild pig showed up one day, and I felt a strange sense of purpose. Feeding these animals gave me a reason to keep going. They made me feel wanted and loved in a way I had never felt before.

I learned every corner of that forest, even in the darkest nights. I could always find my way, and the animals always seemed to find me. But no matter how much I loved the forest, hunger always forced me to return home.

I remember once, I was so hungry that I tried to fish in the lake. I made a stick, stood in the water, and waited. A fish came close enough for me to catch, but I couldn't do it. I just couldn't kill it. I stood there, crying and furious with myself for being too weak to survive. I walked back home, empty-handed, and angry at the world.

Even though life at home was full of pain, the forest gave me a little bit of peace, and for that, I will always be grateful. It was the one place where I felt free, even if only for a short time.

First Suicide Attempt

The first time I attempted suicide, I was very young – still a pre-teen. My parents raised cattle, which inevitably attracted mice and rats to our property. My father kept poison to get rid of them. One day, I took some of the poison. I thought, *This is it. This will end everything.*

Before I did it, I wrote a letter to them. I said, "Thank you for everything you have done for me. But it would be better for me to be dead than alive." I was filled with so much pain and anger.

I took the first spoonful of the poison, closed my eyes, and waited. Five minutes passed, but nothing happened. Frustrated, I took another spoonful, went to bed, and waited again. I kept thinking, *This time, it will work.* But again, nothing happened.

I was so angry. I stood up, kicked the floor, and shouted, "God, you won't even let me die!" I felt trapped, like I couldn't even escape it through death.

The next morning, I told my father that the poison he used for the mice and rats wasn't working. He looked at me and laughed. "You don't know what you're talking about. You're stupid," he said. His words cut deeply, but I didn't tell him what I did.

When I was around 11 years old, something extraordinary happened. One night, I was lying in bed when I heard a voice call my name: "Petronela, Petronela, I am here with you." The voice startled me, and I opened my eyes.

In front of me was a brilliant light, so bright and pure that it filled the room. From the light, a figure appeared, walking slowly towards me. He looked beautiful, and his arms were open as if ready to embrace me. I knew it was Jesus.

He came closer and closer, but I pushed Him away in my heart. I was so upset and angry. I thought, *Why are You here now? Where were You when I needed You?* I couldn't understand why He had allowed me to go through so much pain.

The hardest part was the way He looked at me. His eyes were full of love, but I was furious because, to me, it felt like He had just been watching all my suffering, standing there and doing nothing to stop it. I turned away from Him, rejecting His presence, and eventually, I fell asleep.

That moment stayed with me for years. Even though I pushed Him away, it changed something inside me. Deep down, I knew He was real, and I could never deny that He had revealed Himself to me.

A Summer of Freedom and Questions

One morning, my mother told me to get dressed. I noticed she had packed my suitcase. We got into the car with my father, and as usual, no one said anything during the long drive. We travelled for over three hours before the car stopped in front of a large building. It was an institution: a rehabilitation centre.

I recall that I was about 12 at the time. She took out the big suitcase and handed it over. As I stood there, confused and unsure, a beautiful lady approached me with the warmest smile. She welcomed me kindly, but I had no idea what was happening. My mother turned to me and said,

"You'll be staying here for the holidays."

It was a psychiatric rehabilitation centre, but I didn't understand much of it at the time. Inside, I wanted to jump and shout with joy because I knew this meant I wouldn't be beaten for the next two months. But I kept still, hiding my feelings because I couldn't show any emotion in front of my mother.

My parents signed some papers and left without explaining anything to me. The beautiful lady, who was a nurse, took my hand and introduced me to the other children. When I saw them, my excitement grew. I realised that, for once, I wouldn't have to live in fear.

The centre was for young teenagers with challenging behaviours. Many of the children there were from foster homes, and we all shared something in common – we were seen as difficult, unwanted, or burdensome. But to me, these children weren't difficult or unwanted. They were special. They became my friends, my brothers, and sisters.

For the first time, I felt a sense of belonging. Every day was filled with activities, and I discovered that I could laugh and play without fear. Those two months felt like the best holidays of my life. I didn't want it to end.

On the last day, I cried so much. I hid myself in a wardrobe because I didn't want to leave. The nurse who had taken care of me was so kind and gentle. She treated every child with respect and love, and I wished I could stay with her forever.

When my parents arrived to take me home, I was happy to see them, but deep down, I felt a heavy sadness because I knew what awaited me. I knew the beatings would start again. As I said goodbye, I wanted to cry, to run and hug the nurse, but I couldn't move. My mother stood beside me, watching, and I knew better than to show emotion in front of her.

At home, I was raised in a religious environment. My parents sent me to church every Sunday, but they only attended twice a year on Christmas and Easter. I believed in Jesus. I believed He was real. But I also carried the memory of rejecting Him the night He appeared to me, calling my name.

Even as a child, I had many questions about faith. I often asked the priests why they taught us to pray to Mary when the Bible didn't say to do so. I questioned why we weren't taught to pray directly to God. My questions were unwelcome.

The priests often removed me from class for "causing trouble." One day, I asked a priest directly, "Why are you teaching us to pray to Mary when it's not in the Bible? Isn't that a lie?" He dismissed me, saying, "You're just a child. You don't know anything."

His words hurt deeply. Looking straight into his eyes, I replied, "I'd rather leave this place than accept your lies." He told me to leave the class, and I walked out without hesitation.

I shared with others about the night Jesus came to me, but no one believed me. They laughed at me, calling me a liar. It hurt, but I refused to let their disbelief change what I knew to be true. I carried the memory of that night, of His voice calling my name, as a secret in my heart. It became something I held on to, even when the world around me didn't believe.

New Passion Discovered

At age 14, I asked my mother where my real mother was. Her response was a slap across my face. I didn't move or cry. I stood still as she frowned at me with her cold, blue eyes and said, "I am your mother."

I looked back at her and replied, "No, you're not my mother. You know that." Her expression hardened, and she said, "Your mother is dead."

Summoning all my courage, I said, "That's not true. My mum is alive, and I will find her." She punched me, slapped me again, and screamed, "You are the worst child ever. I adopted you!"

I shouted back, "I didn't ask for that!" She slapped me harder, and I collapsed to the floor. She grabbed a wooden stick and started hitting me with it. I closed my eyes tightly, repeating to myself, "Be strong. One day, I'll find my mother."

One day, I went to the park with my best friend, Ivana. We saw a girl, about 10 years old, fall from her wheelchair. She fell hard, and I immediately ran to help her. The wheelchair was heavy, but I didn't care. I had to help her. As I lifted her back into the chair, our eyes met, and she smiled at me. "Thank you," she said.

That moment filled me with so much joy. Later, her carer came over and thanked me too. I felt needed, like I'm valuable. The girl, whose name was Susan, said, "This is my best day ever." Her words stayed with me.

As Susan and her carer left, I felt so proud. I thought to myself, "This is what I want to do – help people with disabilities." I wanted to run home and tell my mother, but I didn't. I couldn't trust her, and I was still scared of her.

Inside, though, something told me, "Well done."

At the same age, I started learning to play the guitar through a friend from church. It became a passion, and I often went to church just to practice or listen. For my 15th birthday, my parents gave me a guitar. I was so grateful. I wanted to hug them, but I didn't dare. Instead, I immediately began practicing and writing songs.

Playing the guitar made me feel like myself. It was my escape, my joy. But my mother never asked me what I was learning or encouraged me. She would close the door and leave me alone.

One day, after an altercation with my mother, my father, who was drunk, came into my room. He took my guitar, broke it in two, and threw it on the ground. "Don't play anymore," he said. "You're playing it wrong."

I screamed, "No!" and cried, "I'm sorry!" But he walked away, leaving me with the broken pieces of my guitar. I was overwhelmed with guilt, feeling as though it was totally my fault. After that, I stopped playing altogether.

Christmas was the hardest time of the year. I didn't like it because everything in the house felt cold and empty. One Christmas, I hoped my parents would give me a TV game console. When I saw the gift under the tree, I was so happy and grateful.

The next day, I started playing, but my mother came in, took it from me, and said, "You will never play this again." I was shocked and confused. I didn't understand what I had done wrong.

"I'm sorry," I said, but she took the console away.

Anytime I showed joy or excitement about something, she would take it from me, saying, "That's not for you. You don't deserve it."

Even though they gave me gifts at Christmas, I hated the holiday because it always ended with disappointment. I counted the number of Christmases I had left to endure before I could leave. Each one felt like another test of my strength.

Through it all, I kept telling myself, "Just survive. You'll make it." And that thought kept me going.

Another Suicide Attempt

I ran away again, determined to end my life. I decided I would jump from the bridge this time. Before I left, I wrote another letter to my parents.

That morning, on my way to school, I walked across the bridge. I stood there, looking down at the water, and told myself, *If I jump now, it will all be over.* But then another thought came to my mind: *If I die now, I won't see my best friend, Ivana, again. I won't get to eat the lovely food from school.*

Somehow, that stopped me. So, I decided to wait until after school.

When I got to school, I looked everywhere for Ivana, but she wasn't there. I felt so disappointed. I thought, *I can't die without seeing her one last time.* Later, she came back to school after being away sick for so long. Seeing her made me happy, but it also made me sad because I had already decided that this would be my last day.

Ivana was my best friend, and she gave me some of the happiest moments of my childhood. I could talk to her about anything, and she always listened to me. She never told me to stop talking, and I loved her for that. After school, we often walked hand in hand, jumping and laughing together. She made me feel loved in a way no one else ever did.

I cherished the times I spent at her house too. Her mother was kind and always made the best food. Being there felt like an escape from my mother. Sadly, she only allowed me to visit Ivana two or three times a month.

I was about 14 years old when I made this plan. I

decided it would be my final day. I said to myself that dying would finally bring peace to my parents, and it would end my suffering. That day at school, I said goodbye in my mind to my classmates. I remember it clearly. As soon as class ended, I ran towards the bridge.

The bridge stood about five metres above the river. Without thinking, I jumped. But the water was too shallow. I hit the riverbed, soaking wet but still alive. I stood up, cold and furious with myself. I screamed at God, "You won't even let me die!" The freezing water cut through me, but the anger burned hotter.

I climbed back up to the bridge, dripping wet, and walked home. I knew what was waiting for me. My mother wouldn't care what had happened. She wouldn't ask why I was wet. And I was right. When I got home, she grabbed me, slapped me across the face, and started kicking me while I was still soaked.

When she was finished, I crawled to my room, exhausted. The letter I had left to say goodbye was gone, but nothing had changed. I knew more beatings would come, especially in the middle of the night. So, I hid under the bed, curled up, and cried myself to sleep. I was sleeping in bed when a voice woke me up (for a while, I believed I was dreaming).

In my dreams, I saw my biological mother. I thought, *If I die, I'll never find her. I'll never see her.* And so, the cycle began again. I started planning my next attempt, but always with that small hope in my heart. *What if I can find her? What if she is waiting for me?* That thought kept me going, even when I wanted to give up. I fell asleep again.

Reflections: You Are Not Alone in Your Pain

Life can feel unbearably heavy when pain and rejection weigh on your heart. The lies that whisper, "You are not wanted" or "You are better off gone," can echo louder than the truth. But you are not a mistake. You are not forgotten. Even in the darkest moments, when it feels like there is no one to see you or hear your cries, there is One who does.

The Bible reminds us in Psalm 139:13-14, "For You formed my inward parts; You covered me in my mother's womb. I will praise You, for I am fearfully and wonderfully made" (NKJV). You were created intentionally, with love and purpose. Your life is not an accident. Every fibre of your being was designed by God, and He sees value in you, even when others fail to.

You are not defined by the rejection of others or the painful experiences you've endured. There is hope and healing waiting for you. Take one step, even if it is small, towards believing that your life matters, that you are seen, and that you are deeply loved by the One who created you. Keep holding on.

Being Me

Being me is seeing others happy.
Being me is dancing with joy.
Being me is allowing myself to cry.
Being me is painting and creating.

Being me is smiling and laughing freely.
Being me is helping someone stand again.
Being me is praying and talking to God.
Being me is knowing what I want.

Being me is admitting I am weak,
So Jesus can strengthen me in my weakness.
Being me is giving to others without expecting anything back,
Knowing God has already blessed me.

Being me is enjoying each day,
Even when life feels stressful,
Because I know peace will follow.
Being me is loving others as Jesus did.

With Him, I am not lost or weak.
Being me is accepting both the beauty and the struggles of life.
Being me is breathing deeply each day,
Free to help others smile again.

CHAPTER 4

Better to Be Dead Than Hurt

One night, I woke up and found my mother sitting next to me. I was terrified, certain she was there to hit me again. Before she could say anything, I said, "I'm sorry. I'm so sorry. I know I'm a bad child. This is all my fault." I quickly pulled my hands up to protect my head, bracing myself for the blows.

But she didn't hit me. She just sat there, and to my shock, she started crying. It was the first time I had ever seen her cry. She didn't say a word, and I was too afraid to ask why. I just stared at her, feeling confused and scared. But in that moment, something inside me shifted. I believed she was crying because of me. I thought it was my responsibility. I convinced myself that she was heartbroken because I was such an ungrateful child and that she had sacrificed so much to take care of me.

From that day, I began to hate myself even more. I felt like a burden to her, like I was the reason for all her pain. I didn't want to be this "bad child" anymore. I started praying to God with anger in my heart. "Please, God," I cried, "let me die. Then my parents can be happy. They won't have to deal with me anymore. Please, God, just let me die."

Sometimes, I would sit on my bed and cry loudly, hoping she would hear me. I wanted her to come in, to see me, to tell me it was okay, that I wasn't a wicked girl. But she never came. I would rock back and forth, swinging in one place, trying to find some sense of peace, but the pain inside was too much. I would scream through my tears, "Yes, I'm a bad child! Yes, I'm nobody!" And in those moments, I truly believed it.

I longed for her to comfort me, to tell me, "Don't worry. I'm here for you." That's all I wanted, even though

I didn't fully understand it as a child. Her silence and absence only made the emptiness inside me grow. I believed I was born as the biggest mistake on this planet. I was filled with so much anger towards God. I couldn't understand why He let me go through this. Why was He just watching? Why wouldn't He let me die? These thoughts consumed me, and the loneliness felt unbearable.

A Moment of Despair

I believed the world would be better without me, and I started thinking of ways to end my life. I wrote a letter to my parents and decided to jump off the roof of my school. I climbed to the top of the tallest building, closed my eyes, and prepared to jump. But as I prayed to God, asking for the strength to go through with it, I suddenly felt sick. My stomach churned, and I started vomiting. I lay down on the rooftop, crying harder than I ever had before.

As I lay there, I noticed a police car approaching. Panicking, I tried to escape but ended up falling from the roof and landing in a tree. I hurt my hand and knee, but I had no other choice but to go back home. When I walked through the door, my mother grabbed me by the neck, pulled my hair, and slapped me. Despite the pain in my knee and hand, I was determined not to show her any weakness.

For once in my life, I found the courage to stand up to her. I looked straight into her cold blue eyes and said, "You're the devil. I don't feel any pain. You can beat me as much as you want." My words enraged her. She took a wooden stick and started beating me harder. I fell to the floor, covering my head and face with my hands, but I stood up again, smiling through the torment. "I don't feel anything," I repeated. She hit me even more, breaking the stick she was holding, then grabbed another one to continue.

I felt her kicks on my ribs and stomach. I couldn't breathe properly and thought, "This is it. Finally, I'm dying." But when she forced me to stand, her slap somehow woke me up. I stumbled to my room, my ears buzzing and my vision blurred. I crawled under my bed, hiding from the world, consumed by a deep hatred for her and an even deeper hatred for myself.

That night, I woke up, walked to the kitchen, and picked up the largest knife I could find. A voice in my head whispered, "Kill her. Kill your mother." I crept into their bedroom, standing in the dark, knife in hand. I moved closer to her side of the bed, raising the knife. But as I stood there, tears streamed down my face. I told myself, "I'd rather kill myself than someone else." I left their room and went back under my bed, filled with anger and despair.

Through all the problems, I found small escapes in the things I loved. I adored music, dancing, reading, and writing poems. I even won competitions for art, poetry, and drama. My mother hung my certificates on the wall, but she never told me, "Well done." She never praised me, and neither did my father. I loved performing in school plays and dance recitals, but they never came to watch me. Their absence made me feel even more unwanted.

As a child, I joined many clubs – basketball, art, drama, chess, and even maths. I loved all of them because they gave me a reason to stay away from home. On Fridays, I attended art club, where my teacher, Darina, became a beacon of light in my life. She encouraged me, supported my creativity, and taught me so much. I will always be appreciative to her.

At school, I had a moment of hope when I brought home a letter requesting £3 for a school trip. I showed it to my mother, but instead of understanding, she punched, slapped me and accused me of lying. The next day, during the parent-teacher meeting, the teacher mentioned the trip cost in front of her. She shot me a furious look, and I knew I would face her wrath again at home. But I stayed silent, too scared to speak out.

My mother always presented herself as kind and loving to others, but at home, she was a monster. When visitors came over, I was sent to my room, away from everyone. I could hear their laughter from behind the closed door, but I was never allowed to join. In my mind, I laughed bitterly at how fake she was and told myself, "One day, I'll give her an Oscar for this performance."

Even though I felt so small and invisible, I held onto the little joys in my life – the clubs, the art, the laughter of others. Those small moments gave me a flicker of hope in a world that often felt too dark to bear.

Confidence and Childhood

Confidence is the feeling of self-assurance that comes from trusting in one's own abilities, qualities, and judgement. For children, confidence is like a seed that grows when it is nurtured by their environment. This environment includes their family, school, and the broader world around them. When a child experiences love, encouragement, and guidance, they develop a strong foundation of self-worth.

Children build confidence when they are given the freedom to explore, make mistakes, and learn without fear of harsh criticism. Simple phrases such as "well done" or "I believe in you" can have a profound impact on their sense of self. On the other hand, constant negativity, neglect, or verbal abuse can cause them to doubt their worth and abilities.

In a supportive environment, children learn that mistakes are part of the learning process. They grow to understand that failure does not define them, but instead offers an opportunity for growth. Positive reinforcement teaches them to face challenges, take risks, and keep trying even when things are difficult.

However, when a child – just like I was – grows up in an environment filled with constant criticism or is made to feel like they are never good enough, they begin to internalise these messages. They may come to believe that their efforts will never be enough or that they are inherently flawed. Over time, this lack of validation can lead to self-doubt and low self-esteem.

It is very important what environment you grow up in because what you receive as a child shapes your adulthood. I am aware that if I do not forgive and accept myself as God created me, I would continue to lie to myself, God, and those around me because I would allow the past with what happened to me to continue to manipulate me and hurt those I love the most. I wanted to be healed. I think everyone wants that because they deserve it, and it is the foundation of a healthy life. Living in lies prevents God from healing us according to His plan. Faith in God helped me heal and accept who I really am and allowed me to heal mentally and emotionally as well.

The role of caregivers, teachers, and friends is essential in building a child's confidence. By acknowledging their achievements, showing patience when they make mistakes, and offering reassurance, adults can help children develop the inner strength to believe in themselves. Confidence gives children the courage to speak up, try new things, and face life's challenges without being crippled by fear of failure.

When a child lacks this foundation, they may struggle with self-doubt, avoid challenges, or withdraw from social situations. Their potential may be hidden under layers of fear and insecurity. But with the right support and encouragement, even children who have lost their confidence can begin to rebuild it, discovering their self-worth and embracing their abilities once more.

How Did I Lose My Confidence?

Since childhood, I was constantly told that I would never amount to anything – that I was stupid and ungrateful. I endured emotional abuse and mistreatment, which completely destroyed my sense of self. I believed the negative words of my adoptive parents because they were repeated so often, and I received no support from them. I tried desperately to make them proud of me, but they never expressed pride or showed any sign of it. As a child, I felt grateful they had adopted me, and I wanted to prove myself worthy of that, but no matter what I did, it was never good enough.

Every slap and hit from my parents caused a fracture within me, and I began to believe I was a nobody. Their harsh words deeply wounded me, leading me to believe I didn't deserve anything good because I was a "bad child." I had to beg for everything, and I lived in constant fear of making mistakes. I came to believe I was unworthy of love because that was the message I received from them.

Because I lacked confidence, it took me a very long time

to achieve my dreams and goals. I didn't believe I was capable or that I had the right to fulfil my dreams and ambitions. There was no one around me saying, "Petronela, you can do it. You have what it takes." I always dreamed of acting in theatre, and when I got the chance, I gave up because I didn't believe in myself. If we don't receive the right and healthy support in childhood, it will manifest in our adulthood.

I carried negative words into adulthood, and they affected me mentally. For many years, I couldn't understand my purpose and believed I was born simply to survive. I wondered, I dreamed, and I tried, but because I had no confidence, I failed many times. These failures broke me mentally and led me to believe that my dreams were impossible and that I was merely fantasising.

Accepting Myself and My Past

Accepting myself also means accepting my past in truth. It is impossible to forget, but healing becomes possible when you face your past honestly. As a child, I thought and acted as a child naturally would, without the understanding or development to grasp many things. I was vulnerable because I was still growing, and that vulnerability became an entry point for pain and harm, which began to shape who I was.

No child deserves to experience violence. As a child, I couldn't protect myself because I didn't fully understand what was happening. But now, as an adult, I can safeguard myself. Back then, I accepted what was given to me, and over time, I began to believe I deserved it. I even confused the abuse with love – a lie I internalised because it was the only form of attention and treatment I received.

Reflection: Restoring Confidence

You need to accept your present situation and recognise that you need help to rebuild your confidence. Be honest with yourself and search for the underlying reasons for your lack of confidence. Faith in God helped me a lot because I prayed for Him to reveal the cause and heal me. He did this through my faith in Him. You need to seek out the root cause of why you lack confidence. When you find it (God will show you if you ask), forgive yourself, but also forgive those who failed to nurture your confidence during childhood. Then, begin reclaiming it.

Forgiving myself took a while because I had to accept that it was good for me. But before that, I had to start loving myself, and this took so long because I didn't love myself at all. I had to face those who didn't love me, forgive them, and also forgive myself for not feeling loved. It was very painful. I cried so much when I realised that I hadn't been loved for so many years as a child, that's more than 20 years. It's so painful, and no one wants to go straight into pain when they know it will hurt. Your actions will reject it because you don't want to go through the pain, so I started avoiding it. I'm still in the process of forgiving myself. I'm very proud and very grateful to God (for being with me) that I started working on it, with faith. I'll never forget when I was on my knees, crying so much, and I said, "God, teach me to love myself." With this prayer in my heart, I accepted the truth that I didn't love myself, but I needed help to do so.

When you discover the root cause, it will be painful, because you'll realise that the person who was meant to give you that foundation failed. But everyone deserves confidence. I believe with all my heart that God restored my confidence because I asked Him for it, and He also provided me with the tools necessary for life so I could pursue my dreams and never give up.

It took me many years to decide that I truly wanted to know my "self," and I sought God's help through prayer while also using various tools, including therapy, to heal. But I had to go through the pain of discovering the root. If we experience rejection from childhood and grow accustomed to it, it's incredibly painful, as childhood trauma forms deep wounds. Through faith, I learned to accept myself, forgive myself, and heal. This became a blessing, as God not only restored my confidence but also blessed me with other gifts. However, the healing had to come first, so I could raise my children properly and fulfil His plans.

I am still on that journey and will never give up. I am learning to understand what it truly means to be a confidant or to possess true confidence, especially since, in the past, I didn't love or value myself. I wasn't given that foundation during childhood, and as a result, I believed it wasn't something I was entitled to.

By opening my heart to faith in God, Jesus Christ, and the Holy Spirit, I realised that confidence is part of fulfilling God's will for each of us. However, we must be humble to seek help. As Proverbs 16:18 reminds us, "Pride goes before destruction, and a haughty spirit before a fall" (NKJV). Pride can be dangerous and lead to downfall, as it creates a barrier that prevents God from fully healing us or equipping us to live according to His will.

Weirdo

I'm a weirdo to many people.
I hug trees, I dance with the wind, and I talk to God.
I'm a weirdo to many people,
But I don't mind their criticism.
Let them love their world.
I don't mind when they call me "crazy."
I don't mind when they say, "She's the one who believes in Christ."
I know they don't understand – they are just blind.
The proud mock me,
But their hearts are filled with lies and dust.
Their hearts are broken and unhealed.
And I call on God to help them,
Just as He helped me – He never forgot me.
I'm a weirdo to many people when I walk in Your ways, my Saviour,
But I understand them.
God, You let me feel the same pain they carry.
Their hearts are so broken,
The same pain of rejection I've known.
Please, God, have mercy on all of us.
We act like this because we lack love.
We're filled with so much pain and harm.
Please, God, bring Your mercy into our lives,
On every brother and sister.
You love us all.
Your evidence is Your Son, Jesus Christ.
You created everyone – even a "weirdo" like me.
And You never gave up on me – or any of us.

CHAPTER 5

A Life of Pain and Desperation

One morning, I woke up and felt wet. My heart started racing as I panicked, thinking, "Oh no, I've wet myself again. My mother will kill me." I looked down, and I saw blood. I didn't understand what it was. I just knew I would be in trouble, so I tried to hide it. I changed my underwear, but the blood kept coming. Confused and scared, I thought, "Maybe I'm finally dying."

I quickly grabbed a piece of paper and started writing a letter to my parents. I always wrote letters like these when I thought my end had come. "I'm so sorry," I wrote. "I'm such a bad child. Thank you for everything."

As I was writing, she came into my room without knocking. She never knocked. I froze in fear as she looked at me angrily and barked, "Come to the toilet." I was confused because I didn't need to use the toilet. I was also frustrated because I thought she was interrupting my death.

When I reached the bathroom, she threw a sanitary pad at me and said, "Put that on." My hands were shaking so much that I couldn't do it properly. I wanted to cry, but I knew I couldn't because she hated tears. If I cried, she would beat me. I did what she said, but I put it on the wrong way. "You're so stupid," she snapped.

Those words hurt me more than her slaps ever did. I believed it. I believed I was the stupidest, most worthless child in the world. I didn't comprehend what was happening to my body until later when I learned about it at school.

As my body started to change, I hated how my breasts began to grow. I believed I was turning into an animal – a monkey, as my parents often called me. To stop my breasts from growing, I secretly tied a bandage around them. I despised myself so much that I wished I could be a boy. I started calling myself Peter and even stole boys' clothes from school to wear on my way there.

I believed that if I had been born a boy, what happened to me would never have happened. I wanted to be a boy so that no one would ever touch me again, and I didn't want anyone else to harm other girls. I believed that as a boy, I would be stronger, able to protect both myself and those around me. But this thought only deepened my self-hatred, and over time, I found myself despising who I was more and more.

I learned to lie to myself from childhood, and in doing so, I felt at least somewhat heard. As a teenager, I began developing stronger feelings for girls, but I was constantly confused. I fell in love with the lie that I was Peter, and although I knew I was lying to myself, it helped me survive to the point where I started to believe it. I convinced myself that if I were a boy, and later a man, no one would hurt me. I believed I had found my true self by hiding behind Peter.

For many years, I concealed the lie as though it were the truth, to the point that I fully believed it.

At school, I became a fighter. I beat up boys who teased girls, believing I was protecting them. But inside, I was fighting my own battles. The teachers started calling me a rebel and "tomboy." I was so confused, but I started to like it because through it, I began to feel some attraction, experience love, and feel loved by this confusion. I felt free and liked myself this way because I was different.

One day, my mother discovered the bandage I had used to hide my breasts. She was furious. She beat me harder than ever. I felt so exposed. She had found out my biggest secret.

The next morning, she woke me up and told me to get dressed. My father joined her, and they took me to the car. They didn't say a word. I wasn't allowed to ask questions, so I stayed silent. The car stopped outside a big building. I looked up and saw the name: "Psychiatric Ward."

I wanted to ask why we were there, but I knew better. We walked into the building, and my mother never looked back at me. She was always a few steps ahead. In the waiting room, I heard someone call my name. It was the first time I had heard someone say my name with kindness.

The doctor smiled at me and asked, "How are you?" I was so shocked by her kindness that I froze. I glanced at my mother, knowing I had to behave. Later, the doctor said she needed to speak to her alone. I sat in another room and could hear her crying. She was telling the doctor how bad I was and how much trouble I caused.

I wanted to run to her and apologise, but I stayed frozen in my seat. The doctor then called me in to speak privately. My mother glared at me with her cold, blue eyes and said, "Go in." I went in, but I lied about everything. I told the doctor that she was kind to me. I knew I had to, or I would pay for it later.

When we got home, my mother locked me in my room after beating me again. "You're a liar," she screamed. I went to bed hungry, as always, and believed I merited it. I thought, *I am a liar. I am the problem.*

The guilt was overwhelming. That night, I found my

father's razor in the bathroom. I sat on the floor and cut my wrist. Blood started dripping, but before I could process it, she walked in. She screamed at me, punched me in the head, and kicked me while I lay on the floor.

"I'm sorry," I cried. "I'm so sorry." But she didn't stop. She dragged me by my hair, forced me onto my knees, and placed a piece of wood under them. I had to kneel there for hours, unable to move. If I did, she slapped me.

When it was over, she locked me in the basement. It was dark, cold, and full of rats. But the rats became my friends. I talked to them and cried with them in the darkness.

Sometimes, I slapped my own face over and over again, trying to feel something, but I felt nothing. I hated myself so much. Eventually, I cried myself to sleep.

One day, I woke up, and my mother strangely told me to get dressed. I was so happy because I knew we were leaving the house, and for once, she wouldn't hit me. It was the start of summer holidays, a time I dreaded because it meant no school, no teachers, and no classmates – the people I loved so much.

My father drove us a long way that day. I sat quietly in the car, listening to my mother complain. She was calling my auntie and uncle horrible names, saying terrible things about them. My father told her to stop but soon turned to me and said, "We're going to visit them in Košice."

I felt a spark of excitement. I loved visiting my auntie and uncle. They were kind to me, and I adored their daughters, Renata and Henrieta, my cousins. However, I couldn't understand why my mother was talking so badly about them when we were on our way to their house. I felt confused but pushed those feelings aside because I was so happy to be going.

When we arrived, I was overjoyed when my auntie said I could stay for a short holiday about 3 to 5 days. It was a small escape from my life at home, and I wanted to make the most of it. I spent the day drawing, using the pencils my auntie had given me. At one point, I accidentally drew on the blanket. My auntie was furious with me, and I felt so ashamed.

The next day, when my parents came to pick me up, my auntie told them what I had done. I wanted to explain that it was a mistake, that I didn't mean to do it. But I knew no one would believe me because, to everyone, I was just a liar. So, I kept quiet, hating myself for yet another mistake.

When we got home, my mother beat me for it. She slapped me, screamed at me, and called me names. Later, as I hid under my bed, I punched myself, over and over, trying to punish myself for being so improper. I believed everything was my fault. Every bad thing that happened, every mistake – I thought it was all because of me.

Two weeks later, my auntie and uncle came to visit us. I was so excited to see them, but my mother sent me back to my room. From under the bed, I could hear them arguing. My father was fighting with his sister, my auntie. I felt horrible, convinced they were fighting because of me and the blanket I had ruined.

I wanted to run to my auntie and tell her how sorry I was. I wanted her to know I didn't mean to make her angry. But I knew I wasn't allowed to leave my room. So, I stayed hidden, crying silently.

After the fight, my auntie and uncle left. They never visited us again, and I never went to visit them, as I was so sad because I adored Renata (now I know I wanted her attention), my oldest cousin. I always felt amazing next to her; she was like an older sister to me. My mother came into my room, dragged me out by my hair, and slapped me across the face. "You're the black sheep of the family," she said, "and it's all your fault!"

I believed her. I believed that I had destroyed their relationship – that I had caused a rift in the family. The guilt ate away at me, and I started hurting myself even more. I hated myself for the pain I thought I had caused. To me, everything was always my fault.

I had nothing and had to just go and run away to the forest and kill myself again. So I wrote the letter to my mother: "Goodbye, thank you for everything." When I was outside, I saw the police officer, and they found me. They told me that my parents had been in a car accident. I was so shocked and immediately asked, "Are my parents okay?"

The police officer told me, "Yes, your father just hit his head, but they are fine. The car is completely crushed." I think I was about 14 when the police wrote back to me, to my parents. I was so happy to see them, and I was very grateful to God that they were alive. I wanted to jump and hug them. I wanted to so badly. I was so happy, but I just stayed frozen next to my mother and father. I was like a stone. I was very afraid to show any emotion next to my parents. My mother gave me a hateful and very cold look, and I knew what would happen next.

After we came home, we closed the door, and she immediately slapped me and screamed at me. She started punching me. My father spat on me and then left. I started saying, "I'm so sorry, I'm sorry," but she slapped me again. I told her, "I'm so sorry," and she punched me. I fell to the floor, and she started kicking me in the back and the belly. I said, "I'm sorry, I really am sorry." She said, "Because of you, we could have died." I said to her, "But you didn't, you're still alive." She slapped me harder.

I went back to my room and held back my tears, not

wanting her to see. I went back to my room, and I hated myself more and more. I said to God, "Thank You that You protected my parents and myself," and I believed that it was my fault they had the accident.

Are you Struggling with Identity?

Throughout my childhood, I was confused about who I was due to the abuse I experienced, and I had no one around me who believed me. As a result, I grew up living a lie in order to survive, and I hated myself so much. No one was there to tell me, to explain that *this was not my fault.* It is deeply painful when a child, who is still unconscious of themselves and developing, experiences sexual abuse. In order to survive, I lied to myself and took all the blame, which severely damaged my mental health and healthy development.

Anyone who does not want to accept themselves is someone who has not yet healed. They lie to themselves as a coping mechanism, and although it may feel better temporarily, that lie eventually shapes how they see themselves and those around them. What helped me was when I began to be honest with myself and with God. Of course, I asked God, *Where were You when I was abused?* For many years, I was angry with Him, believing He didn't care and had allowed it to happen. But over time, God showed me the truth; it wasn't as I had thought.

God gave us all free will, and it is up to us how we use it. Unfortunately, humans often abuse this free will, causing harm to others. By accepting what happened to me and acknowledging the abuse, I began to see myself the way God created me from the beginning. God gives us a choice: to accept the truth or to hide from it. When we hide from it, we live in a lie. But accepting the truth can be painful because we must confront the reality of what happened. Still, it's necessary for healing and survival.

For a long time, the lies shaped me, and I believed them. But I made the decision that I didn't want to live a lie anymore. I wanted to live in the truth, even if it hurt. As the Bible says in John 8:32, "And you shall know the truth, and the truth shall make you free" (NKJV). That's exactly what happened in my life. By accepting the truth of who I am and what happened to me and by forgiving those who hurt me, I opened the door for God to heal me. Slowly, He began to restore me, making Petronela the person He intended me to be from the beginning.

Now, after years of healing, I see that it was necessary for me to live in the truth so that I could raise my children in a healthy way which is being honest with myself and accepting who I am. Through this journey, I have learned that truth, even when painful, is the path to freedom and healing.

Reflection: When Lies Wound Deep

Lies can cut deeply, especially when they come from those we should trust or when they paint us as something we are not. Being called a liar or being blamed for things outside of our control can create a sense of helplessness and confusion. For anyone who has experienced this, it can feel like your voice is lost, and your truth is buried under the weight of falsehoods.

But the truth is, our worth is not determined by what others say about us. God sees beyond the lies and labels. He knows the deepest parts of us – our pain, our struggles, and our heart's cries. In Isaiah 41:10, the Lord promises, "Fear not, for I am with you; be not dismayed, for I am your God. I will strengthen you, yes, I will help you, I will uphold you with My righteous right hand" (NKJV).

To those who have been misunderstood, falsely accused, or made to feel less than human, know this: God's love is constant and unchanging. He knows your truth, and He calls you His own. The lies of others may try to break you, but with God, you can rise above them. You are not defined by their words, but by the truth of who you are in Him.

No matter what people perceive of me or think about me,
I always shine through at the end of the day, holding onto the hidden victory within me.
I've had many people try to tear me down, to put me down.
But I'm still here, still alive.
Some are even surprised that I'm still breathing,
still living in this world.
I've always been myself, with God's grace and help,
because He created me this way,
and for that, I am truly grateful.
I've made so many mistakes,
and I've had no one to support my dreams.
But I always believed that I could carry on – even if I was alone –
I tried to handle it all by myself.
Once again, I find myself on my knees,
where no one sees me, but God sees my heart.
And again, I ask Him,
"Lord, how long must I endure this attack?"
When the devil accuses me, I scream and cry,
"I'm so sorry!"
But deep in my heart, it hurts so much.

CHAPTER 6

Silent Pain

There comes a point in life when the weight of everything you've carried becomes unbearable. You start to wonder where you belong, who you really are, and if the dreams you hold in your heart will ever have the chance to grow. For me, this chapter was about reaching that breaking point; about searching for freedom and love, even when it felt impossible to find. It's a chapter of rebellion, heartbreak, and, above all, the hope of finding my true family and a place where I could finally belong.

I was meant to take an important exam for high school, but I couldn't do it. I knew the answers; I knew exactly what I needed to write. But I stared at the paper and left it blank.

When I handed it back to the teacher, I could feel the weight of what I had done. It wasn't because I couldn't succeed – I just didn't want the life my parents were forcing on me. They had dreams of me becoming a doctor or a lawyer, but I had dreams of my own.

When we got the results, they were furious. My father was silent for a moment, then he began crying. I had never seen him cry. It shook me, but before I could say anything, he slapped me hard across the face. I fell to the floor, and before I could catch my breath, he started kicking me in the stomach.

"Why would you do this to us?" he shouted.

My mother just stood there, watching. She didn't try to stop him. When I finally managed to stand up, I gathered my courage and said, "I want to be an artist."

My father's face twisted with anger, and he slapped me again. "You'll never make money as an artist," he shouted. "You're a fool!"

Those words hurt more than the slaps. His disappointment cut me deeply. I ran to my room and hid under my bed, trying to escape the shame. My mother followed me, grabbed me by the hair, and started beating me. She didn't stop until she was out of breath. My father left the house, and when he came back later that night, he was drunk. I believed it was my fault. I thought he drank because he was ashamed of me – ashamed of the daughter who had ruined everything.

I felt so guilty, so broken, that I began planning to end my life again. But instead of going through with it, I started writing in my diary. Writing was my escape. I poured out all my feelings – my pain, my anger, and even stories of affection that I created to feel something good. In one entry, I wrote about falling in love with a boy from my school. I used his name and described how much I liked him.

One day, my mother found my diary. She read every word, and when she finished, she confronted the boy, embarrassing me in front of him. I wanted to disappear. I was so ashamed and began to hate myself even more.

She controlled every part of my life – what time I came

home, how I sat, how I ate, even how I stood. If I didn't sit or stand "correctly," she would beat me with a stick. I couldn't breathe freely around her.

But writing letters became my lifeline. I wrote hundreds of letters to my best friend, Ivana. She always accepted them without judgement, and so I kept writing. I poured out my admiration for her as a friend, my dreams, my fears, and everything I wished I could say out loud.

One day, my mother stormed into my room and started slapping me. I was so confused. Then I saw it – a letter in her hand. It was meant for Ivana, but she had read it. In the letter, I wrote about how much I hated her, how I dreamed of surviving and leaving her forever when I turned 18.

She held the letter up and shouted, "You are the worst child! You're a disgrace to this family!" Her punches followed her words, and each one felt like it was breaking a part of me.

But even as I lay there, bruised and destroyed, I held onto one thought: "I will survive. I will leave this place. I will find my mother."

I started counting the days and years until I was an adult. Freedom felt so far away, but it was the only thing keeping me alive.

At 16, I began smoking marijuana with my schoolmates. It wasn't something I was proud of, but for a little while, it helped me escape. When I smoked, the pain and fear disappeared. I laughed in a way I hadn't in years. It became my secret escape, a moment of relief in a life that felt like it was constantly closing in on me.

I knew it wasn't right, but it was the only thing that made the days bearable. As I smoked, I dreamed of the day I would finally be free – free to find my real family, free to be the person I wanted to be, free to live without fear.

After school, one of my schoolmates offered me marijuana, and when I smoked it, I felt like I was flying. I felt so free. When I got home, my mother slapped me straight away and said, "You are drunk." I laughed so much and told her with a big smile on my face, "No, I'm not drunk."

She punched me again, but I laughed even louder. The

more I laughed, the angrier she got. She grabbed me by my hair and kicked me, but I just kept laughing. My mother got so mad and shouted, "You are crazy!" I laughed again and stood up, still smiling, and said, "You can do it again."

At that moment, my father came and punched me so hard that I blacked out. When I opened my eyes, I felt his hands on me, and blood was running from my nose. He punched me again in the stomach and swore at me before walking away, leaving me there.

That day, I felt an even stronger desire to have more drugs. When I was high, I didn't feel anything, no matter what my mother or father said or did to me. Drugs became my escape, my way of coping. They felt like hope, taking me to another world where everything was perfect.

I started searching for more drugs because they gave me the strength to survive. When I smoked, I felt like I could leave all my pain behind. Smiling and laughing became my way of surviving, even if it was only through the haze of the drugs.

Relocated to a Psychiatric Ward

One morning, my mother woke me up and told me to put on my clothes. I was happy because I knew we were going out. I was confused, however, because I was supposed to attend school, yet they didn't tell me where we were going. I sat quietly in the car with my parents. They didn't speak to each other during the long drive. After what felt like hours, we arrived at a huge building. I looked up and saw the sign: "Psychiatric Ward."

I was shocked. I couldn't believe they had brought me to an adult psychiatric ward. I was 17 at the time, and I felt so disappointed. But deep down, I thought to myself, "At least it's better to be here than with them."

When we entered the waiting room, two men in white coats came and grabbed me. They gave me some tablets, and I started screaming, "Please don't leave me here!" My parents didn't even look at me. They signed some papers and left. I watched them go without saying a word, and my heart sank.

The men took me to a room, removed my clothes, and

handed me hospital pyjamas. I screamed and tried to resist. I didn't want them to touch me. I cried out, but eventually, they gave me an injection, and I fell asleep.

When I woke up, I saw a nurse standing near me. I tried to move, but I couldn't because my hands and feet were chained. Panic set in, and I screamed as loud as I could, hoping someone would come to help me. The nurse came back, but instead of untying me, she gave me another injection. Once again, I fell asleep.

The next time I woke up, the chains were still on, and I started crying. I called out, "God, please help me. Please help me." Suddenly, I felt a strange peace wash over me, a peace I had never felt before.

Three days later, they finally removed the chains. I wanted to stand up and go to the toilet, but as I tried to walk, I tumbled. I was certain someone had caught me, as I felt hands holding me steady. I looked around to thank them, but there was no one there. I started to believe I was losing my mind – that maybe this was why I had been sent here.

Over time, I got to know the nurses and the other patients in the ward. I pretended to take the tablets they gave me, hiding them under my tongue and throwing them away when no one was looking. I told myself I had to stay strong because soon I would leave and start looking for my mother.

Despite everything, I found joy in the psychiatric ward. I made many friends, and we all had something in common: we were broken. I loved being with them. It felt like a safe place where no one judged us for who we were.

There was one room in the ward that always caught my attention. I often heard screaming coming from it, and no one was allowed to go inside. I was curious and wanted to know who was there and why she screamed so much. One day, I decided to see for myself.

When I opened the door, I saw a huge bed with metal bars around it, almost like a cage. Inside was a girl, chained at the hands and feet. She was screaming uncontrollably. When our eyes met, she stopped.

I walked closer to her, smiled, and introduced myself.

"Hello," I said. "I'm like you – crazy. But it's nice to meet you." She struggled to speak, but we somehow understood each other. In that moment, I started to care deeply for her.

A nurse found me in the room and told me to leave. As I walked away, the girl, whose name I later learned was Martina, began screaming again. I turned back to her and said, "Don't worry. I'll be back."

For the next three weeks, I spent every night sneaking into her room. I would bring her stolen food, read her poems, and draw pictures for her. She became my best friend, and whenever I was near her, she became calm. I wanted to make her happy, so I did everything I could to bring her some joy.

I learned that Martina had been abandoned by her parents and had struggled with mental difficulties since she was a child. My heart broke for her. I told her, "I understand why you feel this way. You want your mother back, just like I do."

Martina had no family, no friends, no one to care for her. I made it my mission to be there for her, to show her love and kindness. In her, I saw a reflection of my own pain and longing. I promised her that as long as I was there, she would never feel alone.

I told Martina that I wanted to understand how she felt, being locked behind bars and chained all the time. So, I came up with a plan. I started screaming and acting crazy, copying my friend. I learned so much from watching her. Eventually, they locked me in a similar room, chaining my legs and hands, and put me in a bed surrounded by bars.

At first, I thought it was fine. I rested on the first day and thought it would be easy. But by the second day, I realised how boring and unbearable it was. I started thinking to myself, "How stupid am I to have done this?" So, I decided to act normally again. Once they released me, I went straight to Martina and told her, "Now I understand how you feel. I'm so sorry for you – it's awful and boring in there." From that moment on, we became even closer, truly best friends.

Everyone in the psychiatric ward told me I shouldn't be friends with Martina. They called her crazy and said I should stay away from her. But I always stood up for her. I told them, "No, she's not what you think she is. She's my best friend." I didn't care what people thought of me. In a way I had never experienced, I felt proud and brave to stand up for someone. I was so grateful to have her in my life.

Martina was 20 years old, and I was constantly thinking of ways to make her feel better. One day, I came up with a plan to free her. I managed to take the nurse's key after making sure she was asleep. I ran to Martina's room and unlocked her chains. For the first time, we hugged each other, and I started crying because I was so happy to see her free. We looked at each other and began jumping up and down on the bed, laughing and celebrating.

I had stolen a slice of pizza from the bin and saved some popcorn for her, and we had the best night ever. Seeing her smile made me feel amazing. But I knew I couldn't leave her unchained for long. With a heavy heart, I had to lock her back up before the nurse woke up. It was one of the hardest things I've ever done. I returned the key quietly, and the nurse didn't notice anything.

The next morning, I woke up eager to see Martina again. But when I went to her room, she wasn't there. I panicked and ran to ask the nurse where she was. They told me Martina had been transferred to another psychiatric ward. I felt a wave of shock and heartbreak. I ran to the toilet and cried, knowing I might never see my best friend again.

I didn't even get the chance to tell her thank you – for loving me just as I was. She had been the first person to make me feel seen and understood.

After Martina left, the doctors decided it was time to release me too. They told me there was nothing wrong with me. Although I felt relieved, I didn't want to go back to my abusive parents. I couldn't face that life again. So, I started acting crazy once more. I copied everything Martina had taught me.

My plan worked. They locked me up again, and I was happy to stay another week in the hope that Martina would return. But she never did.

Reflections: Finding Light in Darkness

This chapter speaks to the profound loneliness and rejection one can feel, yet it also highlights the resilience of the human spirit and the search for belonging. It reminds us that even in the darkest places, kindness, and connection can create moments of light and hope. Martina's story shows how a simple act of compassion can break through pain and despair. Even when the world seems to reject us, there is still a glimmer of light to hold onto.

One of the key lessons from this chapter is that friendship and compassion have the power to heal, even if only for a moment. Being brave enough to love someone who others have abandoned is a reflection of God's unconditional love for us. It reminds us that we are never truly alone.

This chapter also shows the importance of standing up for others, even when it's not the popular choice. Despite what others said, standing by Martina was an act of courage and faith. It teaches us that loving others as they are is one of the greatest gifts we can give.

We also learn that hope, even when small, can keep us moving forward. Holding onto the dream of finding family or creating a new one, and believing in a brighter future, can carry us through the toughest times.

Proverbs 3:30 says, "Do not accuse anyone for no reason – when they have done you no harm" (NKJV). This verse gives us hope that God sees every injustice and values truth above all. For anyone who has been falsely accused or treated unfairly, know that you are not defined by those lies. God knows your heart, and His truth will always prevail.

False accusations often make us question our worth, but in God's eyes, we are seen and loved. The moments of kindness I experienced in the psychiatric ward, especially with Martina, were reminders that even in the darkest places, God provides people who reflect His love and care. Hold onto those moments and trust that God is always working to restore what has been broken.

Warrior Child

I came like a star in the night sky,
Prepared for knightly armour even before birth.
Born into this life,
Instead of peace, I received a fight for my life.
Rejected in my mother's womb,
Betrayed by my own family from a young age.
I felt like Herod's child,
Cast aside and forgotten.

The devil whispered, "A coincidence child."
But he didn't know – God had chosen me.
He called me into this world to fulfil His will.
Through pain, I would come to understand His purpose.
"You will search for Me for many years, My child," God said.
"The devil will try to dwell in you for a while.

But do not worry –
You will find Me, My child."
"I placed knight's armour upon you from the start.
I took your parents from you,
Even knowing you would hate Me for a while,
Screaming, 'How could You?'"
"But I gave you a reason to seek Me.
I filled your heart with a desire –
A longing from the beginning."
And so, I was born,

Silent Pain

A child with a healthy body,
Eyes that searched,
Ears that listened.
I looked for my mother and father,
But no one cared to see the source of my pain.
I came to understand that, in this world,

I would be alone for a while.
Even in my anger,
Deep within, I kept a hidden love –
A determination to find my mother,
To uncover the truth of what had happened.

A wandering child, weary with fatigue,
Dreaming of an end to the suffering.
But still, I composed another poem,
A small act of defiance,
To survive another day,
Even when the pain seemed too much to bear.

CHAPTER 7

Divine Intervention and Turning Points

Life often brings moments where we feel trapped in darkness, unsure of how to move forward. One morning, I woke up to the sound of screaming. My heart sank immediately, and I froze in fear, wondering what I had done wrong this time. I didn't even know what was happening, but instead of saying "Good morning" to my mother, I instinctively said, "I'm sorry, I'm sorry." She didn't reply. Instead, her hand struck my face, and I fell to the ground.

She started shouting at me, "Why did you put food under the bed? Why are you such a bad child? Why would you hide food that I prepared?" Her words were harsh and filled with anger. Before I could even speak, she punched me in the neck. I wanted so badly to explain, but I was too afraid to tell her the truth.

The truth was, I wasn't hiding food to waste it. I was saving it for my tiny friends – the mice that lived under my bed. They would come out whenever I had cheese, bread, or scraps. I loved them. They weren't afraid of me, and I spoke to them all the time. They felt like my only friends in the world, and in their small way, they gave me comfort.

But my secret didn't stay hidden for too long. One day, my mother found one of the mice. She caught it in front of me, and I watched in horror as she killed it right there. I screamed, "No!" but before I could do anything, she slapped me again and sent me back to my room.

I crawled under my bed, hiding from her, and cried harder than I ever had before. My heart broke because my friend was gone. The one creature that gave me a sense of love and connection was taken away. I hated her even more that day.

But as I lay there under the bed, I knew I had to survive. I started making plans for my future. I promised myself that when I turned 18, I would leave my parents forever. I held onto that hope, counting the years, months, and days until I could finally escape.

For many years, that thought kept me going. It became my light in the darkness, my reason to endure. I didn't know what the future held, but I knew that one day, I would find freedom and begin to live the life I had always dreamed of.

I counted the days and years until I would turn 18 and finally be free. Each night, as I lay in bed, I whispered to myself, "Just survive." Deep down, I knew what my mother was doing to me was wrong, but I believed I deserved it. I thought I was a mistake, a devilish child. I cried only when I was alone, speaking to my tiny friends, the mice I called Robert and Funny. They gave me comfort in a way no one else could.

At school, I was known as a happy child. I wanted people to see me that way because making others smile gave me a reason to live. Seeing someone laugh because of me filled me with joy and honour. It was the opposite of what I felt at home, where I couldn't be myself.

Sometimes, I just wanted to sing or dance in my room, but my mother would scream, "Stop it! Stop it!" I stopped, but deep inside, I still felt grateful that she and my father had adopted me. Even though they told me I was a mischievous child, my heart was thankful.

The Big Day: Freedom at 18

The big day finally arrived – October 6th, my 18th birthday. I jumped out of bed with excitement, knowing that today was the day I had been waiting for over the past ten years. I told myself, "This is the best day ever." At school, I told my classmates, "Today, I'm leaving my parents for good." After school, I came home, and my mother called me into the kitchen. She had prepared a birthday cake. But when I told her I didn't want it, she became furious – she threw the entire cake in the bin. My father sat silently in his chair, not even looking at me.

I stood up, gathering all my courage, and said firmly, "I'm leaving you both today." My mother, enraged, reached out to slap me, but I caught her hand mid-air and looked into her cold, blue eyes. I told her, "Never again – you will never touch me again." Never before in my life had I stood up for myself. I was amazed by my own strength, and for a moment, I saw the shock in her eyes – a mixture of anger and disbelief.

My father finally spoke: "Go." I went to gather my belongings, but my mother stopped me, saying, "You're not taking anything with you. Nothing here belongs to you." As I headed for the door, my father looked me in the eyes and said, "You'll end up as a prostitute – you're an animal, not a child." I looked back at him and replied, "You're wrong, and I'll prove it to you." He opened the door, swore at me, and slammed it shut as I stepped outside.

It was dark, cold, and windy, but I felt liberated. "Yes,

I'm free," I whispered to myself as I ran to the forest – my safe place. I found a large tree, covered myself with leaves, and fell asleep. The next morning, I woke to the sound of birds singing. It felt like the most beautiful morning of my life. I was truly free like never before.

I felt hungry, so I went to the village and searched for food in bins. I found some bread and ate it quickly, tears streaming down my face. "I'm free," I cried. "My mother will never hit me again." My mother will never hit me again, and I won't call her "Mum" again. I hated calling her that all these years because I knew she wasn't my mother, but I was forced to call her "Mum." I hated it so much and resolved to calling her "stepmother." It was the first day in years that I didn't hear anyone telling me how worthless I was. I returned to the forest and back to my tree.

Later, I knew I had to retrieve my ID, so I went to the police station and told them that I had left my parents' home and needed my ID. They accompanied me to the house, where my mother greeted us at the door. The police officer explained that I was there to collect my ID, but my mother claimed they didn't have it. My father backed her up, saying, "We already gave it to her when she left."

I stood there, holding back my tears, and told the officer, "They're lying." My mother then told the officer I was a troubled child and had been sent to a psychiatric ward multiple times. She even showed them documents to support her claim. I felt defeated – the police laughed and didn't believe me. I left silently, tears welling up as I watched the police car drive away.

I ran back to the forest, knowing I couldn't survive there long-term. I couldn't bring myself to harm the animals to eat, so I returned to the village, sleeping in parks and searching for food in bins. Despite everything, I still felt relief – I was free from the abuse.

One day, while sitting in a park, a man approached me and asked if I wanted to earn money. Desperately needing it for my ID, I agreed. He led me to a house, gave me vodka, and explained what I needed to do. I took three shots, closed my eyes, and did everything he asked. As I lay there afterwards, I whispered to myself, "My father was right." I hated myself even more.

From then on, survival became my only goal. I did whatever it took – sex work, stealing, and sleeping outdoors. Drugs helped numb the pain and kept me warm on cold nights. I often slept in cemeteries, where I felt a strange sense of peace among the dead souls.

My Church Visit

One morning, I woke up shivering, only to find my blanket covered with the season's first snowfall, right in the cemetery. Winter had arrived, and it dawned on me that I needed to do something to survive, to find warmth and safety. I returned to the forest and began sleeping in the hay that was left out for the deer. I taught myself how to make a fire in the forest, and every day, I went back to the village to look for food.

I always knew where to go when I needed help or when I wanted drugs. I did everything I could to find some warm tea or food. Despite everything, I was happy because I was finally free and far away from my parents. I believed they were happy without me. I knew they were aware of my homelessness because people in the town had seen me.

I will never forget the kindness of strangers who didn't judge me but instead helped me. My best friend, Ivana, also did everything she could to support me. She would secretly hide food for me and bring it outside. We would meet behind a car, where she gave me hot tea. I was so grateful to her, and in those moments, I realised who my true friends were. I felt blessed to have chosen someone as loyal and kind as Ivana.

I spent more than two, almost three months living as a homeless person. I survived through drugs and other things I'm ashamed to speak of, but I was relieved knowing my mother would never hit me again. I was happy to be free from the abuse, even though I knew the way I was living wasn't right. That freedom, however, brought with it a growing desire in my heart – a longing to search for my real mother, a dream I had held since childhood.

As time passed, I began to feel ashamed of the things I was doing, but I didn't see any other way to survive. I had no choice but to learn how to live in this harsh new reality. One day, I went to church by myself, looking for a place of peace, a place where I could find God.

I went to church by myself because I was looking for a place where I could feel peace and stay for a while. In the church, I always felt calm and safe. One day, while I was sitting there, a woman looked at me kindly, but another woman gave me an angry look. I knew they could smell the homelessness hovering all over me. They turned their heads and went back to the front of the church. I thought to myself, "They are so hypocritical," but I chose to leave it to God because He is the ultimate judge.

Since I was a child, I always spoke to God as if He were my friend. There were times when I was angry with Him, but there were also moments when I was deeply grateful. Talking to God brought me peace, no matter how I felt or what I said. In the Catholic Church, they encourage people to go to confession, but I hated it. Even as a child, I questioned it. I would ask, "Who is this priest to forgive my sins?"

One time, during confession, the priest told me that my sins would only be forgiven if I prayed five "Our Fathers" and five "Hail Marys." I told him, "That is too long. I can't do this." I also told him that I had met Jesus, and He came to me. I shared with him my biggest secret about how Jesus had revealed Himself to me. The priest called me a liar. I was so upset. I told him, "You have no love for others. You shouldn't even be a priest. My advice to you is to seek God."

I remember when I was much younger, the priest got very angry, and we ended up arguing during the confession. He told me to leave. I said to him, "You have no power to decide if my sins are forgiven. Only God does. You are not God." He shouted at me to go away. I stormed out of the confession room and slammed the door so hard that everyone in the church heard the loud noise.

From that day, I stopped going to confession. I lied to my parents, telling them that I had gone, but I never went. If they asked me what I said to the priest, I would make something up. I avoided that priest after that, and he ignored me whenever he saw me. Later, he was replaced, and I was so happy. As a child, I loved running to church. It was the only place where I felt like myself. They allowed me to go nearly every day.

However, I found the preaching and singing in the church boring. I didn't feel any joy in it. I often wondered, "Why aren't these people happy? What is wrong with them?" I questioned everything, especially the priests who preached. I believed that priests and anyone involved in the church were supposed to be survivors, like me.

I often asked myself why my parents kept a Bible at home but never opened it to read. One week, I gathered the courage to ask them. I asked, "Why do you have a Bible if you never read it?" My mother looked at me sternly and I froze. She replied, "It's not your problem. You don't understand because you're a stupid child."

I thought to myself, *It's just a question*, but after that, I never asked them about it again.

An Unexpected Angel of Hope

One cold winter night, I found myself shivering in the snow. I had no choice but to hide under a car for warmth. As I tried to fall asleep in my sleeping bag, I heard a woman screaming. Without thinking, I jumped up and ran towards the sound. A man was trying to rob her, grabbing her handbag. Without hesitation, I sprang into action. From behind, I leapt onto him like a tiger and grabbed his neck tightly.

The man froze, and I pretended I had a gun by holding up a stick. "Please, man, leave me! Don't kill me! I have a newborn child," he begged. I didn't say anything. I let him go, and he ran away faster than I had ever seen anyone run before. I felt a strange sense of strength and pride as I handed the handbag back to the woman. She thanked me before walking away, and I stood there amazed by what had just happened.

That moment stayed with me. It made me wish I was more masculine, but it also left me confused about my identity and who I really was. I went back to the church because I felt so lost and cold as a homeless person. The first occurrence, I cried out to God, "Please, God, help me find my mother. I need a miracle."

I stayed in the church, hiding between the chairs so no one could see me. When the church closed, I was left alone, completely alone with God. I began to laugh and said, "Thank you, God, now we are alone." I explored every corner of the church, hoping to find some food, but there was nothing. Feeling empty but somehow peaceful, I stood in the middle of the church and began to sing.

I sang loudly for God, and it became one of the best moments of my life. As I sang, I felt an overwhelming sense of peace and joy. I sang more and more, smiling through my tears. Eventually, I fell asleep on the church floor. I woke up early in the morning to the sound of nuns arriving for prayer. Quickly, I ran out of the church to make sure no one saw me. That night was the best I had ever spent, alone with God.

Later, I found someone who gave me marijuana, and after smoking, I wandered to the cemetery. As I walked, I suddenly saw a huge white angel standing near me. The angel came closer, and I thought, *Wow, these are some great drugs.* But as I blinked, the angel turned into my grandmother.

She was holding food and hot tea for me. I couldn't believe it. My adoptive grandmother, at 72 years old, had come all the way to find me. I felt a sense of shame as I took the food and tea from her. I ate everything quickly because I was starving, trying hard not to cry. She looked at me with the most loving and kind expression I had ever seen. Her eyes were full of warmth and compassion.

"Tomorrow, I will come again," she said. I protested, "No, Grandma, you can't even walk properly." She smiled and replied, "God will help me." As she walked away slowly, I stood there in shock, watching her disappear into the distance. Tears began to flow down my face.

I remembered my time in the church when I asked God for a miracle to find my mother. My grandmother's kindness felt like a miracle, a reminder that God was listening to me. The next day, she came again, bringing more warm food and hot tea. I decided not to smoke marijuana that day because I didn't want to disappoint her.

She looked at me and said, "Come to my home. Christmas is coming." I shook my head and said, "No, Grandma, I'm not a good person." She smiled gently and said, "I don't mind. No one is perfect. Please come, at least for Christmas."

It was two weeks before Christmas, and every day, my grandmother came to the cemetery, bringing me food and tea. She was old and had trouble walking, but she came anyway. Her love touched me deeply. I decided that I would go to her house, so she wouldn't have to struggle to walk to me anymore. For me, my grandmother was like an angel. She gave me hope in a time when I felt completely lost.

I was so touched by her actions. I rang the bell, but I stood still when I realised she lived right next to my parents' house. Her house was number 85, and theirs was number 84. For a moment, I didn't know what to do. Then, my grandmother opened the door with a big smile and said,

"I've been waiting for you since this morning."

I went inside, feeling so ashamed because I smelled terrible. My grandmother gently said, "First, take a bath, and then we'll eat." I hadn't had a proper bath in over three months. The moment I got into the warm water, I felt like I was in heaven. I felt clean, reborn, and peaceful in her home.

After the bath, she served me food, and then she said, "Stay here with me. You need to finish high school." I was in my final year, but I told her, "I don't want to be a burden to you. I'm not even your real granddaughter." She looked at me with her beautiful, kind blue eyes and said, "All of you grandchildren are equal to me."

She added, "You can do better, Petronela."

Her words hit me so deeply. I couldn't hold back my tears. I stood up and left her house. I didn't know why, but I was so scared. At the same time, I was deeply touched by what she had done for me. I ran as fast as I could, crying, and went back to look for drugs. I couldn't stop thinking about her kindness and the words she said to me – "You can do better." No one had ever said that to me before.

When Christmas Day came, I had such a strong desire in my heart to see my grandmother again, but I was scared. That morning, she came to the cemetery where I was staying. She said, "Come to my house. It's Christmas. Let's be together."

I couldn't hold back my tears. I started crying, and she opened her arms. For the first time, I jumped into her arms and hugged her tightly. We walked together to her house. That day, I helped her cook Christmas dinner. It was the best Christmas of my life – just me and my grandmother. She gave me socks as a gift, and I was so touched by her kindness and love. We sang together, laughed, and talked. It was the happiest I had felt in a very long time.

Later that night, she asked me to stay overnight. I said yes, and we continued talking and enjoying the Christmas evening. At one point in the night, I heard her talking. I asked, "Grandma, are you okay?" She replied, "Yes, I'm just talking to God." She was praying passionately. It was the first time in my life I had seen someone so deeply and genuinely praying to God. It touched me more than I can explain.

The next day, her daughter Monica came to the house. I stayed in the next room while they talked in the living room. I overheard my aunt saying, "Mum, Petronela can't live here with you. She's a prostitute and an immoral person." My grandmother stood up and said firmly, "This is my house, and I decide who stays here. Petronela needs help, and she is staying with me."

Her daughter became very angry and shouted, "You'll regret this, Mum!" Then she left.

At last, someone stood up for me. I was amazed and deeply moved. After Monica left, I went to my grandmother and said, "I'm so sorry, Grandma. I don't want to cause any problems for you." She simply looked at me with kindness and said again, "You can do better, Petronela."

I couldn't hold back my tears. For some reason, I ran away again. I didn't want to, but I felt like I had to leave. I didn't want to be a burden to her. I went back to the streets.

Reflections: God's Unexpected Helpers

In this season of my life, I learned that God always sends help, often in the most unexpected ways. When I felt completely alone and hopeless, He sent my grandmother as a reminder of His love and care. Her words, "You can do better," stayed with me. Through her kindness and persistence, God showed me that I was not forgotten, even when I felt lost.

Looking back, I see that God was always with me, even in the darkest moments. He used people – like my grandmother and strangers – to bring light into my life when I couldn't see it myself. Each act of kindness was a reminder of His love and a call to keep going.

If you are struggling, know this: God sees you, even in your pain. He will send the right people at the right time to remind you of His care. Trust Him, even when it's hard to see the way forward. You are never truly alone.

I Place it All in Your Hands

I unintentionally place the child – myself – in your hands.
I place my birth in your hands.
Rejected by my mother, I place her in your hands.
I place the missing fathers in your hands.
Taking my first steps without parents, I place them in your hands.
Searching for love, I place that longing in your hands.

I place my suffering in your hands.
I place my desire for love in your hands.
I place my restlessness in your hands.
I leave every unanswered question in your hands.
I place every tear in your hands.
The hatred I feel for myself, I place in your hands.

Heal me, my Lord.
Fill me with your love.
I forgive them, my Lord.
For I've known for a long time that you are my parent, O my Lord!

CHAPTER 8

The Beginning of Redemption

Sometimes, life brings you to a breaking point, a moment when everything feels like it is crumbling. But it's in that brokenness that the first seeds of redemption can begin to grow. For me, it started with a hospital bed, a grandmother's unwavering love, and the realisation that hope was still possible.

When I was homeless on the streets, I often got pneumonia. Many times, I couldn't feel my feet or even my toes. I kept searching for new places to stay warm, but it became harder as the winter grew colder and the snow piled up. I couldn't stay in the cemetery anymore; it was far too cold. I noticed I had a very high fever, and with the last bit of strength I had, I decided to return to my grandmother's house.

With trembling hands, I rang the bell. When my grandmother opened the door, I couldn't stand on my feet anymore, and I collapsed right in front of her. The next thing I knew, I was waking up in a hospital bed. I later learned that I had severe pneumonia. When I opened my eyes, I saw her sitting next to me, holding my hand. She was praying. I felt so grateful to her because I realised she had saved my life by bringing me to the hospital.

I stayed in the hospital for three weeks, and when I was discharged, my grandmother asked me to stay with her. She said, "Please stay in my house. You need to finish your high school." After being homeless for eight months, I moved into her home. I took my studies seriously and started focusing on finishing school. I even enrolled in art school. Thanks to her encouragement and support, I graduated from both high school and art school.

However, her decision to take me in upset my father and mother. They were furious that she was helping me.

One day, I heard them shouting at my grandmother outside her house. They were screaming that she shouldn't let me live with her. My father even said, "You can die outside if you want. You chose Petronela, so help yourself!"

I saw everything from the window and ran outside to help her. She had fallen on the stairs. I helped her stand up. I saw tears in her eyes. She said, "My son is lost. Please, God, forgive him." Tears streamed down her cheeks, and I felt terrible again.

I told her, "It's because of me. The whole family doesn't talk to you because of me. They hate me, and now they've turned against you. It's all my fault."

I started crying and told her, "I need to leave again. I'll go back to the streets and take marijuana." She looked at me and asked, "What is that?" I was shocked that she didn't know what drugs were. She asked me to explain what I was taking and why.

As I explained, she listened patiently, never interrupting. While we talked, I forgot all about my desire to take drugs. She then said to me, "I don't understand everything, but you can do better, Petronela."

Her words stayed with me. I had never met anyone as humble, honest, and strong as my grandmother. She was a simple woman, always smiling, and I never once heard her complain.

One day, I asked her, "Can I bring some of my friends here? They are homeless."

She smiled and said, "Yes, of course."

I brought around twelve people to her house. All of them were homeless. My grandmother prepared food for all of us. We had the best time ever. Some of my friends had a guitar, and we sang songs for her. We laughed, shared food, after a long time, we felt warmth and kindness.

She didn't mind that they were homeless, that they smelled, or even that some were under the influence of drugs. She simply served food to everyone with a big smile on her face. Her generosity and kindness touched me deeply. I was so proud to have a grandmother like her.

The Search for My Mother Begins

My grandmother helped me so much. She gave me all her savings so I could apply for a new ID. I felt bad because I didn't know how to repay her kindness. At that time, the only way I could earn money was through sex work. Later, I started delivering goods to trucks, which also helped me earn a bit more money.

One morning, I woke up and told myself, "Today, I will start looking for my mother." I believed she was alive. I didn't know how I could find her, though. Even my birth certificate only had the names of my parents. I spoke to my friend Peter for advice, and we spent a month doing research, but we couldn't find anything.

All I had was my first name, my true date of birth, and the city where I was born. Believing it was my best option, I decided to go to the council in the town where I was born. Upon reaching there, I said to the lady at the counter, "Good morning. I'm here to find my true mother." She laughed and replied, "That's impossible. You were adopted, and by law, I cannot open the records."

For me, "no" was not an answer. I told her angrily, "I have been waiting for this day for 19 years. I know my mother is alive, and I will find her." She asked me to leave, so I left angrily. I felt hopeless and smoked marijuana to calm down. Somehow, I ended up in a church. On my knees, I prayed, "God, please help me find my mother. I believe she's alive."

The next day, I went back to the council. The same lady saw me and said, "You're back again?" I replied, "Yes, and only you can help me." She asked me to leave, but I told her firmly, "I won't leave until you tell me the truth about my parents' names." She threatened to call the police, so I left, but I told her, "I'll be back."

That night, I slept outside in a park. The next morning, I saw her walking into the council, and I followed her. She saw me and said, "You're here again?" I knelt before her with tears in my eyes and begged, "Please, just let me see my true birth certificate." She looked at me and said, "I have never met someone as stubborn as you."

Still on my knees, I told her, "I just want to find my

mother." She sighed and said, "Maybe she's already dead. What's the point?" I stood up, looked her in the eyes, and repeated what I had told her. She teared up and finally said, "Fine, but it will cost you a lot of money." She told me the amount, and I promised to return with the money.

I had no choice but to return to sex work to earn the amount she had asked for. A month later, I returned to the council with the money. I was so nervous and excited because I knew this was the day I would find out my true mother's name. The lady took me to her office. I handed her the money, and she counted it in front of me. Then she said, "You have five minutes."

I was shaking as I looked at the records. For the first time, I saw my mother's name - Kvetoslava Vasilova, her date of birth, my father's name, and their address. Tears were streaming down my face as I tried to write it all down. My hands were shaking so much, but I managed to copy the details. The lady said, "Five minutes are up. You need to leave." I left and started running. I couldn't stop crying, and I read my mother's name out loud: "Kvetoslava." I thought it was such a beautiful name. I knew I was getting closer to seeing her.

I decided I wouldn't wait. I believed my mother was also looking forward to meeting me. I didn't have much money left, so I hitchhiked. A kind driver offered me a lift and dropped me off in the town where my mother lived. I thanked him and said goodbye. I was so excited. I found the house number and street written on the paper, but when I arrived, I saw an empty, old house in very unsightly condition.

A lady from the next house came out and asked, "Who are you looking for?" I told her, "I'm looking for Kvetoslava Vasilova, my mother. Do you know her?" She said, "Yes, everyone here knows her." I was so happy to hear that. I thought to myself, "My mother must be well-known." The lady continued, "I'll give you the address of her sister, Maria. You should see her first."

I was surprised and thought to myself, *Wow, I have an auntie.* The lady wrote down the address and gave it to me. She asked why I was looking for Kvetoslava, but I told her,

"It's a long story." I thanked her and left.

I kept repeating my auntie's name and address in my mind until I reached the street. I asked a few people for directions, and they helped me. Finally, I rang the doorbell, and someone opened the door. I saw my auntie. She looked at me and immediately started crying, saying, "Petronela." I replied, "Yes, it's me. I'm here to find my mother."

I asked her if my mother was alive. She said, "Yes." I jumped and hugged her tightly. I was so happy and excited. She invited me inside and started explaining what had happened. She said my mother had been mentally disabled since birth. After I was born, my mother struggled with alcohol and homelessness. She often ran away and couldn't take care of me. When I was two months old, she left me outside. Social services found me and placed me in an orphanage.

I asked my auntie why she didn't take care of me. She said she was busy studying and had her own problems. I was shocked to learn that my mother was disabled, but I was also relieved to know she was still alive. I asked for a drink, and my auntie gave me some alcohol. Later, she told me that my father was also mentally disabled. I was overwhelmed by everything she told me.

My auntie then asked, “Are you okay mentally?” I was surprised by her question but replied, “I think I am. Although many people believe I’m crazy.” I stood up and told her, “I want to see my mother.” She warned me, “Be prepared. She drinks every day and might be drunk.” I asked her why the family wasn’t helping her, and she explained, “We’ve tried many times, but nothing has worked.”

I thought to myself, *Yes, she’s my mother because I’m a troublemaker too.* I told my auntie, “I want to see her today.”

Seeing Mother for the First Time

We walked out of the house, and my auntie and I kept walking for about 10 minutes. Ahead of me, I saw a woman lying on the ground. She had long hair and looked like she was asleep. My auntie stopped and said, “That person you see on the ground is your mother.”

I was shocked. My heart raced as I walked straight towards her. I was so excited and couldn't believe I was finally seeing my biological mother. I said to myself, "This is it. I've found her." I knelt down close to her and said softly, "Hello, Mum. It's me, your daughter, Petronela." Tears were streaming down my face.

My auntie just stood there watching. My mother didn't move. So, I said again, this time louder, "Hello, Mum. It's me, your daughter, Petronela." She stirred a little, moving her hand and head, but didn't look at me. Then, in a slurred voice, she swore at me and told me to go away.

I froze. I wasn't ready for this. The pain and rejection hit me like a storm. I started running, tears blinding my eyes. I ran and ran until I couldn't breathe anymore. I stopped, collapsed to the ground, and cried.

I couldn't believe it. My own mother, the one I had dreamed about for years, the one I had waited my whole life to meet, didn't want me. She didn't even care who I was. In that moment, it felt like my life was over. Every dream I had about her, every hope that she loved me and missed me, was shattered. I wanted to die. I felt there was no point in living anymore.

I told myself, "This time, I will do it properly. I've tried to kill myself before, but it never worked. Now, I don't have a reason to keep going. I've found her, and she doesn't want me."

Encounter With the Angel

I made my way to the train station, determined to end it all. It was dark, nearly 11 o'clock at night. I stood there, waiting for the last train. As I saw the train's light in the distance, I closed my eyes. I prayed to God, saying the Lord's Prayer. I whispered, "This is it. I'm finally going to die." The sound of the train grew louder and closer. I stood still, ready to end everything.

Then, out of nowhere, something or someone pushed me off the track. I fell hard onto the platform as the train rushed past me. I was shaking, unable to understand what had happened. When I looked up, I saw a huge white angel standing beside me. It glowed with a golden, sparkling light, brighter than anything I had ever seen. As the angel moved closer, I felt a deep, overwhelming love, unlike anything I had ever experienced.

I thought to myself, *This can't be real. Maybe it's the drugs.* But the angel reached out and touched my head. In that moment, I felt pure love. Tears poured down my face, and I dropped to my knees, crying out, "God! God! What do you want from me?"

I said, "I'm sorry, God. I'm so sorry." I cried and cried, feeling ashamed, but at the same time, I felt loved. I couldn't stop sobbing because I had never believed that someone could make me feel like this. I started to repent, saying, "God, you didn't even let me die. What do you want from me?"

That moment changed me. I knew there was a reason I was still alive, even though I didn't understand it. I fell asleep at the train station that night, and when I woke up early the next morning, I went straight to find some drugs. But something strange happened. When I tried to take the drugs, my hand wouldn't open. It felt like something was holding it shut. I couldn't understand what was happening.

My friends laughed at me, asking, "What's wrong with you?" I told them about the angel and how God had saved me. They laughed even more and said, "You're just making this up." I felt disappointed that no one believed me, but deep inside, I knew the truth.

That moment at the train station stayed with me forever. It was the first time I genuinely believed that God was real and loved me just as I was. Though I still wondered why He chose me – why He didn't let me die – I knew He had a plan. Gradually, my desire for drugs began to disappear. When someone offered me drugs again, I found myself saying, "No." I was shocked. I didn't understand how or why, but I remembered the prayer I had said at the train station: "God, please help me. Deliver me from this."

From that day, I stopped taking drugs. I realised that God had truly delivered me. It was a supernatural moment, one that stayed with me forever. I felt hope.

Return to the Streets

I started living on the streets again. I couldn't go back to live with my adopted grandmother because I felt I needed to be alone. I begged for money outside, and a thought came to me: "Buy a rope, go to the forest, and hang yourself." Without a second thought, I went and did just that.

I believed in my heart that God had saved me before, that He had sent an angel to rescue me, but I couldn't understand why. I felt I had no purpose in life. After my biological mother rejected me, I returned to my favourite place – the forest. I tied the rope around a branch and then around my neck. I closed my eyes and jumped. But the branch broke. I was so angry, tears streaming down my face, and I screamed to God, "What do you want from me?"

I left the forest, knowing that if I told anyone what had happened, they wouldn't believe me. I was so certain that admitting I had attempted to kill myself would only lead to me being sent me back to the psychiatric ward. I felt like I was going crazy and asked God over and over, "What do You want from me? What do You want from a broken person like me?"

I had no one to share my problems with, no one to help me with the rejection I was feeling. The pain made me stronger, but it also left me angry with God. I started talking to Him more. I didn't realise it at the time, but He became my best friend. I told Him everything. I respected Him and also feared Him.

One day, a friend invited me to a Christian festival (Campfest). He said, "Come, you'll enjoy it." I agreed, thinking I could bring some beers with me. But he said, "No alcohol or drugs are allowed." I laughed and asked him, "What do people even do there without alcohol or drugs?" He replied, "They worship Jesus and pray." I had nowhere else to go, so I said yes. He bought me a ticket, and I went with my tent for four days.

When I arrived, I walked into the worship area. People were singing a song, "*Bless the Lord, O my Soul.*" As soon as I heard it, I went to my knees and started crying. I felt

God's presence so strongly. After a long while, I felt loved. I said to God, "Forgive me," and I began to repent. I whispered, "Please help me."

A group of seven people came over and prayed for me in tongues. I didn't understand what they were saying and felt very confused. They told me, "You have demons inside you," which made me angry. As they continued praying, I started screaming and vomiting. Then I began crying uncontrollably. I felt something I couldn't explain – something powerful that I couldn't control. I wanted to leave, but they kept calling out the name of Jesus, and I found myself unable to move.

One of them looked into my eyes and said, "You are chosen." I was filled with anger and shouted back, "You're lying to me!" Then I left with tears running down my face. The words "You are chosen" stayed in my mind, and I couldn't stop thinking about them. I didn't believe him because I felt I had no use in life.

The next morning, something woke me up. I felt God's presence again and began to confess, "I'm so sorry, God. I don't know what to do. Please help me. I don't want to live like this anymore." I went back inside the festival, and they prayed for me again. This time, I experienced something supernatural – like a heavy burden leaving my body. In that moment, I became determined in my decision to leave sex work behind.

I realised that if I wanted to live a better life, I had to work. I met a man who was polite and kind. He offered me a job in the Czech Republic. I worked there for nine months and met amazing people. During that time, I fell in love with the man who had helped me. But later, I found out he was married. He had lied to me. My heart was broken, and I felt completely shattered.

By then, I was pregnant. When I told him, he immediately denied the baby was his, insisting it was possible. His rejection hurt me deeply. I had no one to turn to, and I felt so ashamed. I decided to have an abortion. After it was done, I looked down on myself even more.

I tried to numb my pain with alcohol. I bought a bottle of vodka, locked myself in a room for three days, and drank while crying. I believed God despised me for what I had done. I had killed my child. I convinced myself that I wasn't capable of being a mother – that I would never be responsible enough to raise a child. I thought about my own childhood and told myself I didn't want my child to go through what I had experienced. So, I justified my decision by thinking it was better this way.

But the guilt consumed me. My father's words echoed in my mind – that I was worthless and would never achieve anything. I felt so empty inside. The dismissal I had faced from my mother and this man broke me completely. I believed I didn't deserve life.

Drunk and broken, I tried to kill myself again. But I didn't have the strength. Deep down, I knew that if I tried, God would stop me again. This thought made me even angrier – with myself, with God, and with the world. I started drinking even more to escape it. I was lost, hopeless, and drowning in rejection.

A New Chapter Awaits

One of my very good friends from the Czech Republic, Ivana, told me, "Come with me to England. You can work as a nanny and take care of children." At first, I said to her, "But I don't speak English." She replied, "Don't worry. They will give you food and accommodation. All you need to do is take care of the children."

I didn't fully understand everything, but I knew I had to leave and run away from the place where I couldn't stay anymore because of everything I had been through. So, I said, "Yes, I'll go." Ivana helped me with the paperwork, and I decided to return to Slovakia to see my grandmother before leaving.

When I arrived, I was so relieved to see her after such a long time. I told her, "I'm going to England, but I don't have any money." She gave me £50, and once again, I felt so grateful. This woman had helped me so much throughout my life. I wanted to leave quickly, but before I did, she prayed for me.

I asked her, "Grandma, why do you pray so much?" She

looked at me with her kind eyes and said, "I pray because I believe that one day, you will pray like me." I laughed and told her, "Grandma, that will never happen."

When the day came for me to leave, my heart felt heavy. I knew I had to go, but it was so hard to say goodbye. As I stood up to leave, she said, "Let me pray for you one more time." She prayed, and when she finished, I said goodbye with tears in my eyes, but I hid them from her.

Then I heard her say to me, "I love you, and I know you can do better." Her words touched my heart so deeply. I hugged her tightly, trying to hold back my emotions. I quickly let go and left before she could see me crying. I glanced back one last time and saw her standing there. I knew I had to go.

I got on the bus and started my journey. It was a 22-hour trip, and as I sat there, I felt a mix of emotions – excitement, hope, and a little fear. But deep down, I believed that something better was waiting for me in the United Kingdom.

This journey, everything I have shared so far, is just

part one of my life's story. A story of struggle, survival, and searching for purpose and identity.

But my journey didn't end here. Moving to the United Kingdom marked the start of a new chapter, a chapter filled with fresh challenges, unexpected opportunities, and life-changing experiences. It was a place where I began to truly discover myself and my purpose, even as I faced new trials along the way.

Part two of my story – my life in the UK – is in my next book. In it, I share how I began to rebuild my life, find hope, and see God's plan unfold in ways I could never have imagined.

Thank you for joining me on this journey so far. I hope it has touched your heart, and I invite you to stay with me as the next chapter unfolds.

Reflections: God Is Real

This experience at the train station was a life-changing moment that proved to me that God is real and that His love is beyond anything we can imagine. In my darkest moment, when I had given up hope and was ready to end my life, God intervened in a way that no one else could. He sent an angel to save me, not just physically but spiritually as well.

I had always questioned if God truly cared about me. I thought I was too broken, too far gone for His heart. But in that moment, God showed me that His love is unconditional. He didn't save me because I was perfect or deserving; He saved me because He is a loving Father who never gives up on His children.

The supernatural encounter with the angel was a reminder that God is active and present in our lives, even when we feel abandoned or unworthy. It was also a turning point that sparked my journey of repentance and healing. God showed me that He had a plan for my life, even if I didn't understand it yet. Psalm 46:10: "Be still, and know that I am God; I will be exalted among the nations, I will be exalted in the earth" (NKJV).

If you are struggling to believe that God is real, remember that He often reveals Himself in ways we don't expect. Sometimes, it's in the smallest act of kindness; other times, it's in life-altering moments like mine. God loves you, even when you feel unworthy, and He has a purpose for your life. Trust Him, and let Him guide you into His light.

The Last Goodbye

The last goodbye I gave you,
It is better to live without bread than to live without you.
Do you remember the stars we shared together?
Even our God above could not boast of a love like ours.

The last goodbye, for the hundredth time, I told you:
Perhaps it is better to live without the sun than to live without you.
God crept into my dream, but I chased Him away,
For I was born in sin, and sin taught me to cry.

I have lived in pain,
But I have also learned to love.
I kept climbing from the withered tree,
Struggling to survive a life without love,

A life without you.
I was so lost, so broken,
Abused and forgotten without you.
I don't know how, but still,
I am calling on God:
"Please help me."

CHAPTER 9

Choosing to Never Give Up

Every journey is filled with lessons, struggles, and moments of clarity. It is often through our darkest seasons that we discover our greatest strength. For me, the path wasn't easy, but every step taught me something new about life, faith, and resilience.

What kept me going when everything felt hopeless? How did I find light when my world seemed consumed by darkness? These are questions I've often asked myself, and now I want to share the answers with you.

In this chapter, I will reflect on the most important lessons I learned through my journey, how my faith in God became the foundation of my strength, and why forgiveness and letting go are essential to healing. I'll also leave a message of hope for anyone who feels like giving up and offer guidance on how to find the strength to keep moving forward.

This chapter isn't just about my story; it's about the power of faith, perseverance, and redemption. If you've ever felt broken or lost, my hope is that these reflections will inspire you to never give up and to discover the purpose and strength that already lie within you.

Let's take this step together – because your journey is worth it.

My Life's Greatest Lessons

What was the most important lesson I learned from my journey? I discovered that, whatever I wanted in life, I had to find out for myself if it was truly right. Since childhood, I lacked proper support and love, which left me vulnerable and caused me to make many mistakes. Without the nurturing guidance of a mother or anyone to reassure me, I learned to survive instead of truly live.

I carried this survival mentality into adulthood. I couldn't accept myself because I never had anyone tell me it was okay to make mistakes. I believed I had to be perfect, but I didn't understand that everyone makes mistakes. There were days when I didn't want to live, as I couldn't see any meaning in my life. I believed I was destined to achieve nothing.

Despite everything, I clung to the hope that one day I would experience true love. That hope kept me going. I knew I couldn't live in a violent environment forever, and my dream of finding my mother and being happy with her drove me forward. I truly believed that if I found her, my life would be complete. This belief taught me to never give up and to remain determined in reaching my goals.

Throughout my journey, I faced many obstacles that caused me to lose control at times. In my deepest moments of despair, I cried out to God for help, and He heard me. Slowly, I learned to communicate with Him and trust Him more each day. My faith in God grew stronger, and it saved me. It gave me the strength to keep going, and through

Him, every dream I had began to take shape.

The most important lesson? There are so many. Each one is important in its own way because every lesson taught me something valuable. Every challenge brought me closer to my goals, and for that, I am deeply grateful.

I learned to accept life as it is, letting go of regrets about the past. Instead of being trapped by my mistakes, I began to learn from them. I came to understand that God has forgiven me through Jesus Christ – a powerful and unconditional love that covers all of us. I discovered the power of honest confession, recognizing my sins and weaknesses, and trusting that God would help me overcome them.

Although it sometimes took me years to let go of my stubbornness, I realised that each step brought me closer to the person I was meant to be. And for that, I will always be thankful.

How God Strengthened Me

Today, after 40 years, I know that without faith in God, I would not be here. I have come to realise how blessed I am to have received faith in God. Through this gift, God communicates with us and helps us. I opened my heart to Him, and in doing so, I was honest about who I was. When I accepted Jesus Christ into my heart, I was a prostitute, and I carried so much shame, but He accepted me just as I was.

Looking back, I now understand why I made the choices I did in the past. I didn't value myself or see the worth that God has given each of us. I believe that God placed the right desire in my heart – the desire to find my mother one day – and He used that to help me survive the darkest times when I was bullied, abused, unwanted, and rejected.

Faith in God began to transform me, shaping me into the person He created me to be. At the same time, my faith started to heal me, little by little. Faith in God is a journey that takes time because it's through this journey that we truly get to know Him. Through my faith, I developed a personal relationship with Jesus Christ and learned how to communicate with the Holy Spirit.

Faith in God revealed His incredible love to me, shown through the sacrifice of Jesus Christ – the greatest act of love for all humanity. My faith changed me so much that now I can look in the mirror and say, "Thank you, God, for what You created."

Through faith, I learned to never give up. For me, faith is like the fuel in a car – without it, the car cannot start. My faith in God, in Jesus Christ, and in the Holy Spirit has become the foundation of my daily life, and I cannot imagine living without it. I am deeply grateful because my faith in God has saved me many times. For that, I thank God with all my heart.

A Message of Hope

We all face struggles in life. Difficulties and challenges are a part of everyone's journey. There isn't a single person on this planet who is always happy or always sad. Life is full of ups and downs, from childhood to adulthood. The most important thing is how we handle these moments.

I often failed to handle situations in life because I didn't have the support or guidance I needed. There was no one to tell me, "You are not alone, Petronela." For me, the hardest times were when I felt completely alone. I desperately wanted to be loved and wanted, but when I didn't get that attention, I felt like giving up on life.

This feeling of loneliness is something many who are suffering understand too well. When people feel alone and abandoned, unsure of how to move forward, they may lose the will to live. Loneliness can feel like it is suffocating you. Those who are in despair often don't realise their value or see the gifts they have.

Many times, people suffer when they are betrayed or abandoned, and in their pain, they lose sight of hope. I know this feeling because I went through it myself. I wanted someone to tell me there was a way forward, and I found that way through being born again.

What does it mean to be born again? At first, I didn't

understand how I could be born again when I was already alive. But for me, being born again means changing your way of thinking, forgiving yourself and others, accepting what has happened, and starting fresh. It means opening your heart to faith in God, accepting Jesus Christ, and thanking Him for dying for us. It means humbling yourself and asking God to forgive your sins and mistakes.

When you do this, you will be born again. You will realise you are no longer alone. From that moment, you can face every difficulty and every joy in life because God will be with you. With His help, you can overcome anything. That's what I did, and my life became lighter. I now have a Helper. I can't see Him, but I know He is there, and He is more precious and blessed than I ever imagined.

If you are hurting, don't keep it inside. You need to be honest about your pain and bring it to God. That is the only way to change things for the better. Confess your struggles to Him and start working on them with His help. God has given us tools to guide us, and one of the most powerful is His Word – the Bible – which teaches us and equips us for every challenge we face. You are never truly alone, and with God, there is always hope.

2 Timothy 3:16-17: "All Scripture is God-breathed and is useful for teaching, rebuking, correcting and training in righteousness, so that the servant of God may be thoroughly equipped for every good work" (NKJV).

Why Is It Important to Forgive and Let Go of Pain?

Faith in the Lord Jesus Christ has taught me many things, and one of the greatest lessons is the importance of forgiveness. Through faith, I discovered who I truly am. It was through God's love that I learned to forgive – even when it seemed impossible – and this forgiveness brought freedom to my heart and mind. Faith showed me that I am special, and this love is not just for me but for everyone. We are all valued by God, who gave us His most precious gift: His son, Jesus Christ.

When I believed in Him, I started to seek Him and discover who He is. It took many years, but faith humbled me and completely transformed my life. God freed me from the bitterness I carried, healed my wounds, and changed my heart. Through faith, I began to understand that His love is limitless, and because of this, I was able to love others – even those who had hurt me. God became my closest friend, and our relationship continues to grow every day.

Through prayer and trust in Him, I realised that forgiveness is not just for others – it is for ourselves. Without forgiveness, there can be no inner freedom. When we hold on to pain and resentment, we remain trapped in the past. But when we forgive, we release the heavy burden of anger and bitterness, allowing ourselves to heal. Forgiveness is not about excusing the wrongs done to us; it is about freeing ourselves from the control of those wrongs. This is what Jesus taught us through His sacrifice on the cross.

When I accepted Jesus Christ into my heart, I cried for two days. The realisation of what He did for me overwhelmed me – someone who had never met me physically died for me. I understood that only a love as pure and selfless as His could accomplish such an act. That love convicted me and helped me understand that I didn't want to live in sin anymore. Through faith in God and Jesus Christ, I experienced deliverance and freedom from many spiritual battles. I felt God's power in my life, and it became clear that forgiveness was a part of His plan for my healing.

Faith also helped me recognise that God had already forgiven me. For a long time, I struggled to accept His love because I didn't believe anyone could truly embrace me. But through His word, prayer, and the Holy Spirit, God showed me that I was worthy of His love and forgiveness. He also sent people into my life who helped me when I was at my lowest, reminding me that I am never alone.

Forgiveness is not easy, and it takes time, but it is essential for inner peace. When we forgive, we are not only obeying God's will but also allowing His love to work through us. It is through forgiveness that we find freedom, healing, and the strength to move forward. God desires for us to live in the fullness of His grace, but that requires us to let go of the pain that holds us back.

Taking the first step towards forgiveness is a powerful decision. For me, it came through faith in God. If you are struggling to forgive, I encourage you to turn to Him, ask for His help, and trust that He will guide you. God's love is the key to forgiveness, and through Him, you can find the freedom and peace you seek.

He revealed His grace to me – and through that – He showed me that the life I was living wasn't right. I believed that only He, Jesus Christ, could help me – but first, I had to surrender and allow Him to heal me. With patience and compassion, He made me see that my feelings of rejection and being unloved stemmed from deep-rooted pain caused by sexual abuse and abandonment. He taught me that healing begins when we make the choice to live rightly and embrace what is good.

I regretted – deeply and sincerely – the way I had been living. As a prostitute, I cried out, "Help me," and that cry marked the first step towards change. I realised that acknowledging my mistakes and admitting I needed help was key to transformation. You need to be honest with yourself – that's the only way to uncover the root of your issues and begin the journey towards healing.

I carried many burdens (drugs, homelessness, and mental health struggles) because I didn't have the right role models growing up. Rejection and violence left scars, but through faith, I discovered that it is possible to leave the past behind and live a new life filled with peace.

Through my faith in Jesus Christ, I was willing to surrender myself fully to Him. Now, I understand that my struggles had a purpose – so that God could transform my struggles into strength. He can do the same for you if you are willing to face your pain and trust Him to guide you.

For me, faith in Jesus Christ brings daily transformation – He rescued me, healed me, and helped me overcome what seemed impossible. Praise God for that! Jesus' sacrifice on the cross revealed that true love is forgiveness, and forgiveness flows from loving both God and others.

Christ's example of forgiveness inspires me daily. I aim

to show love by forgiving those who hurt me, while also seeking forgiveness because I know I am not perfect. I believe that when I forgive others, God forgives me too. Forgiveness is a daily choice – one I have embraced, and you can too.

Never Give Up!

It is very important to know where your strength comes from and who gives it to you. I confess my faith in God, and I firmly believe that my strength comes from Him. I am deeply grateful for this and fully accept it. His strength has helped me in every situation in my life.

Growing up, I did not have a family, sister, or brother to turn to during my most difficult moments. This lack of support meant I didn't have anyone to guide me with the right advice. However, as my faith in God grew, it began to help me immensely. Day by day, I learned to trust God more and believe that He wanted the best for me – that He truly loved me.

Choosing to never give up is a decision we face daily,

especially in challenging situations. With a firm decision and the right foundation – Jesus Christ, who will never leave us – it is possible to persevere. You will find strength in knowing that the One who is in you is stronger than the one in the world. It's important not just to talk about this faith but to live it. By refusing to give up, your actions will reflect the power of God working within you.

God gives His strength to those who ask and truly desire it. Each of us has free will, and it is up to us to decide to seek Him and ask for what we need to face life's challenges. Many times in my life, I felt I was no longer in control, but when I was honest about my struggles and cried out to God, He was glorified in my life by giving me the strength to carry on. I believe God's will for each of us is to live in a way that pleases Him, but to do that, we must first seek Him and accept Him into our hearts. Only you and God know the condition of your heart, and He is waiting for you to invite Him in.

As a child, I deeply longed to be valued. I believe everyone does because love is essential for healthy development. When I didn't receive affection but instead the opposite, it shaped me into a stubborn person who learned to survive and fight. As I became an adult, I carried all my unhealed traumas into my life, which made me more vulnerable. But I thank God that He saw my heart through it all. He never abandoned me and showed me His love.

I longed for love, and I found it through Jesus. People told me He was the only way, so I started searching to see if it was true – if someone had really died for me. I didn't know Him personally at first, but when I chose Jesus Christ, my entire life changed. He healed me and gave me everything I had missed in my childhood. The most beautiful gift was realising that He died for me – on the cross – for my sins and weaknesses. He chose to suffer for me, and He endured it all for everyone, not just me. His sacrifice has made Him the most well-known name in the world, and it is because of His great love.

In the Bible, I found many stories of people who never gave up and endured until the end. Their stories inspire me, and I believe I can endure too because I know where my strength comes from – it comes from God. You can find this strength as well. You just need to want it, ask for it, and believe in it.

Choosing to never give up is a decision you make every day.

Choosing to never give up means being willing to stand up, even when you fall.

Choosing to never give up means fighting through the darkest moments.

Choosing to never give up is about letting the light within you shine for the world to see.

Never give up – you can do it, because you are chosen. You are still alive, and that is proof that your story isn't over yet!

Silent Call in Secret

Been away so many years from home,
No one understands my soul.
Trying to find love through my mistakes,
I know I've been so hopeless, so lost.
Crying and shouting filled that night,
O, I couldn't understand. How did I survive?

Tears kept falling down.
A touch came too close, too soon.
As a child, I didn't realise
A monster was there to destroy my soul
The child named Petronela.
She stood there, drinking, watching me,
My eyes begged her silently, Help me. I'm just a child.
But she drank more,
Closed the door,
And watched as he entered.

The man lied to me with hollow words,
His actions carved scars that stayed.
Through every touch,
He planted envy, fear, and shame inside.
I wanted to run,
But I froze like a stone.

Oh, as a child, I wasn't strong!

No strength to flee,
No courage to scream,
I didn't understand the evil around me.
With their act they are just lost souls who abused me.
I cry and don't want to breath anymore.
Oh no and no again,
I can't run away.
I don't understand much but it's hurting me,
No one here to protect me.

About The Author

Petronela Zilik is a resilient and inspiring individual whose powerful memoir chronicles her tumultuous journey from a troubled childhood to becoming a dedicated charity leader. Born into a life of adversity, she was separated from her mother at just two months old and spent her early years in foster care before being adopted at the age of eight. However, despite finding an adoptive family, she did not receive the love and support she needed. At the age of 18, she made the brave decision to leave an environment of domestic violence. The scars of her early experiences shaped her reality, leading her to live on the streets, where she faced unimaginable hardships, including homelessness, drug addiction, and a life of prostitution. These cycles of despair repeated for years.

Petronela's life took a pivotal turn when, after two decades, she located her biological mother. However, this long-awaited reunion brought further heartbreak when her mother rejected her. This profound disappointment pushed Petronela into a dark place where despair loomed large. Yet, against all odds, she found the strength to rise from her struggles, driven by a relentless spirit and a deep desire to make a difference in the lives of others.

With a diverse educational background, Petronela has pursued various qualifications to equip herself to support others on their journeys to healing. She holds a Higher National Diploma from London Churchill College, alongside multiple certifications in psychology, counselling, and advocacy for victims of domestic violence. This extensive training, combined with her life experience, underscores her commitment to understanding and addressing the challenges faced by those affected by trauma.

In 2021, Petronela founded *Petronela's Hope*, a non-profit organisation dedicated to providing support and resources for victims of domestic violence. As the CEO and Director, she has organised numerous fundraising events, including a notable upcoming event in March 2024, all aimed at raising awareness and funds for those affected by domestic abuse. Additionally, she has held exhibitions in Oxford and recorded her own CD, showcasing her artistic talents and commitment to creative expression.

As a single mother of three young children, Petronela embodies resilience and determination. Her unwavering love for her mother, despite years of rejection, reflects her extraordinary capacity for compassion. Through her memoir, Petronela aims to share her story not only to raise awareness about the realities of domestic violence and mental health but also to inspire others to find hope even in their darkest moments.

All proceeds from this book will go directly to *Petronela's Hope*, ensuring that her story not only sheds light on her personal journey but also provides essential support to those in need. Petronela's mission is clear: to empower others and build a community of hope, healing, and love.

For those who wish to connect, support, or learn more about my journey and the work I do through Petronela's Hope, please visit

www.petronelasshope.org

I'd love to hear from you and walk this journey of healing, faith, and hope together.

Thank You for Reading My Book!

Your support means the world to me. I deeply value your feedback and am genuinely interested in hearing your thoughts. Your input will significantly contribute to enhancing my future literary works.

Would you kindly spare a moment to share your insights by leaving a review on Amazon? Your feedback will help me understand your thoughts on the book better.

Thank you immensely for your time and consideration.

Warm regards,

Petronela

Printed in Great Britain
by Amazon

60506817R00111